D0436260

Boundary Issues

Other titles by Jane Adams

Boundary Issues

Using Boundary Intelligence to Get the
Intimacy You Want and the Independence
You Need in Life, Love, and Work

Jane Adams, Ph.D.

WILEY

John Wiley & Sons, Inc.

Copyright © 2005 by Jane Adams. All rights reserved

Published by John Wiley & Sons, Inc., Hoboken, New Jersey
Published simultaneously in Canada

Design and composition by Navta Associates, Inc.

No part of this publication may be reproduced, stored in a retrieval system, or transmitted in any form or by any means, electronic, mechanical, photocopying, recording, scanning, or otherwise, except as permitted under Section 107 or 108 of the 1976 United States Copyright Act, without either the prior written permission of the Publisher, or authorization through payment of the appropriate per-copy fee to the Copyright Clearance Center, 222 Rosewood Drive, Danvers, MA 01923, (978) 750-8400, fax (978) 646-8600, or on the web at www.copyright.com. Requests to the Publisher for permission should be addressed to the Permissions Department, John Wiley & Sons, Inc., 111 River Street, Hoboken, NJ 07030, (201) 748-6011, fax (201) 748-6008, or online at http://www.wiley.com/go/permissions.

Limit of Liability/Disclaimer of Warranty: While the publisher and the author have used their best efforts in preparing this book, they make no representations or warranties with respect to the accuracy or completeness of the contents of this book and specifically disclaim any implied warranties of merchantability or fitness for a particular purpose. No warranty may be created or extended by sales representatives or written sales materials. The advice and strate-gies contained herein may not be suitable for your situation. You should consult with a pro-fessional where appropriate. Neither the publisher nor the author shall be liable for any loss of profit or any other commercial damages, including but not limited to special, incidental, consequential, or other damages.

For general information about our other products and services, please contact our Customer Care Department within the United States at (800) 762-2974, outside the United States at (317) 572-3993 or fax (317) 572-4002.

Wiley also publishes its books in a variety of electronic formats. Some content that appears in print may not be available in electronic books. For more information about Wiley products, visit our web site at www.wiley.com.

Library of Congress Cataloging-in-Publication Data:

Adams, Jane, date.
    Boundary issues : using boundary intelligence to get the intimacy you want and the independence you need in life, love, and work / Jane Adams.
        p. cm.
    Includes bibliographical references.
    ISBN-13 978-0-471-66045-3 (cloth)
    ISBN-10 0-471-66045-0 (cloth)
    1. Interpersonal relations. 2. Personal space. 3. Privacy. I. Title.
    HM1106.A32 2005
    158.2—dc22

                                                            2005003121

Printed in the United States of America

10 9 8 7 6 5 4 3 2 1

Before I built a wall I'd ask to know
What I was walling in or walling out.

Robert Frost, *Mending Wall*

Contents

Self • Fences of Chicken Wire, Wooden Slats, and
Concrete • All or Nothing at All • Locking the
Door vs. Leaving It Open

- When Inside Information Isn't—and When It Should Be
- You and the Corporate Culture—Good Fit or Misfit?
- Triangulating the Boundaries—Pitfall or Policy?

11 When Boundary Styles Collide

What's This Fight Really About? • As Long As We're Fighting, We're Alive! • When Conflict Brings You Closer • When Conflict Drives You Apart • The Difference between Resolving Conflict and Transforming It • How Boundary Style Shapes Your Response to Conflict • Using the Basic Skills of Boundary Intelligence to Cope with Conflict

Acknowledgments

This book would not have been possible without the help of many people. The writings and research of Dr. Robert Kegan, Dr. Nancy Popp, and Dr. Ernest Hartmann inspired me to explore boundaries from a theoretical as well as a phenomenological perspective; Fred Hills helped me clarify my ideas about this subtle and often over-looked concept and was responsible for setting me on the path toward publication; my agent, Ellen Levine, stayed with it, and me, through an arduous journey; and Tom Miller saw the possibilities in my initial proposal and shepherded the book to its final form.

I am especially grateful to Peggy Gilmer, whose expertise as a coach and organizational consultant informs every page; her intellectual contributions are great, but her friendship over thirty years is a gift of even greater magnitude.

Many people helped me develop the Boundary Style Questionnaire through dozens of iterations; they are too numerous to mention, but they know who they are, and I deeply appreciate their patience, forbearance, and assistance.

Boundary issues are a fact of life in friendships and families, and I owe a debt of gratitude for the love and understanding shown to me by my own—especially Peggy, Carol, Barbara, Kate, Jennifer, Steve, Cam, and Jenny.

Boundary Issues

Introduction

Once upon a time when there were no boundaries, so far back that we have no conscious memory of it, we were *one*. Infinite in time and space, floating in a blissful ocean of being. A twitch, a cough, the sensation of warmth or cold, a pang of thirst or hunger—was it hers or ours? It didn't matter—there was no self for it to matter to. There was just *one*.

We can never remember that feeling of wholeness, although mystics, artists, and lovers have tried to recapture it. But for the rest of our life, we will miss it.

Emerging out of that perfect coexistence, stranded forever on the shore of separateness, we encountered the first of many boundaries that would distinguish what was Me from what was Not Me. And for the rest of our lives, we will try to understand it.

Only trace evidence remains in our psyche of that embryonic state of boundlessness, like a fossil outlined faintly in a long-buried chunk of Precambrian rock. We may wonder how or even if something that happened so long ago, for such a brief, forgotten time, can make a difference in our lives today. But the psyche remembers, which is why, as the psychiatrist Margaret Mahler wrote, all human love and dialogue since then have been striving to reconcile our

1

longing for that lost bliss of oneness with our equally intense desire for separateness.

Our minds accommodate these two conflicting needs by the making and unmaking of boundaries—mental structures that increase in number and complexity as we experience other people and develop our own mental capacities.

Physical boundaries enclose the space in which we feel secure. Social boundaries determine our comfort in connection with others. Emotional boundaries define our capacity for empathy, compassion, and mutuality. Ethical boundaries determine the lines we draw between the moral and the immoral, the acceptable and the unacceptable. Professional boundaries distinguish not only what behavior is appropriate with our colleagues and in our workplaces but also the difference between who we are and what we do. And psychological boundaries—which are at the heart of this book— determine how we reconcile that deep longing for intimacy and autonomy, oneness and separateness, and how the struggle to do so dominates our lives and our relationships.

- Will we always (or mostly) be trying to erase the boundary between ourselves and others, or will we (often) be trying to shore it up?

- Will we always (or often) be trying to shelter and protect the self, or will we always (or often) be trying to merge with an other?

- Will we always (or usually) put ourselves first, or will we always (or usually) be serving the needs of other people?

What Boundaries Are and What They Do

Psychological boundaries are the mental lines that format all the bits and bytes of our mental processes—our memories, experiences, thoughts, emotions, sensations, associations, and impulses—to create the inner identity we call the self. These boundaries enable us to distinguish our thoughts and feelings, minds and emotions, from those of others. And while they occupy a territory of mental rather than physical geography, they're no less real than a wall, or a fence, or a border.

Boundaries are the means by which the self knows who it is and who it isn't. They determine not only where *I* end and *you* begin but also the space between us. Boundaries are central to how we deal with the dilemma of being human—the self-in-relation dilemma—which is balancing the need to be close and connected to others with the need to maintain our autonomy and independence.

Boundaries are key to how we deal with intimacy, loneliness, conflict, anxiety, stress, and challenge at every stage of life. They are integral to how our identity is constructed; because they are so central to the development of our personalities, to how we think and feel about ourselves and how others experience us—our inner as well as our shared reality—they provide a special lens through which we can perceive not only *that* and *who* but also *why* we are. Boundaries explain:

- Why we're anxious when someone leaves us, even if he's only going out to walk the dog. Or why we find it easy to fall in love but harder to make a sustained commitment to another person.

- Why we always put the most work into relationships, even with the most difficult people. Or why we avoid someone who knew us when we had zits and braces rather than tell her how much she hurt us.

- Why other people's feelings often seem more real to us than our own. Or why we're such drama queens that we ignore theirs.

- Why we sometimes don't feel we exist unless someone loves us, or why we don't believe it when they do. Why we keep some secrets but not others. Why we welcome confrontation and competition or resist it. Why time seems to tyrannize us.

Why our children and our spouses, and especially our parents, still push our buttons. Why men seem so alien and hard to understand, or other women—certain other women—push a whole different set of our buttons. Why we don't always know when we're full, even if we've just eaten an entire Sara Lee cheesecake. Why we seek relief from loneliness or boredom with drugs, alcohol, sex, or shopping. Why we confuse intimacy with selflessness. Why we have such a hard time saying no and such anxiety about saying yes, or vice versa.

Are Boundaries a Woman's Issue?

Boundaries and *boundary issues* are words we read, say, and hear all the time: Have you tuned in to Dr. Phil or read *O* magazine lately? Been in therapy or recovery or know someone who is? Had someone call you "codependent" when you thought you were just being a supportive partner, parent, or friend? Been told to get out of someone's face when you didn't realize you were in it? But despite our familiarity with the terms, boundaries are actually the least understood and most overlooked element of our psychological and emotional life.

Because boundaries regulate distance and closeness, they influence how vulnerable we allow ourselves to be, controlling not only how open we are with others but also how vigilant we are in protecting our real selves from intrusion or encroachment.

Women often have a harder time with boundaries than men do. We may feel that it's unfeminine or unfriendly to draw a line around a part of ourselves and mark it with signs that warn others not to trespass or at least to tread lightly. We worry that if we make our boundaries clear we'll be perceived as cold, distant, and standoffish. Yet if we don't, we risk losing our ability to be truly intimate with those whom we choose to share our deepest selves.

Boundary is a word that's frequently uttered in the same sentence with *sexual*. That's understandable, because many people think about boundaries in terms of abuse or harassment. Even though women know we have a right to protect ourselves against uninvited sexual advances, we may be less comfortable about claiming our other boundary rights: to separate from our families without sacrificing our individuality or compromising our adulthood; to clarify how close we want to be to friends and colleagues; to deepen our intimate relationships without losing ourselves in the process; to distinguish among our private, public, and social selves; to control our own time; to strike a balance between our longing for connection and our need for separateness.

Boundaries are particularly relevant to women, who are—let's face it—much more at home with feelings and sensitive to the nuances of emotion than most men. That's due as much to our upbringing, traditions, and the culture that shaped us as it is to the neurobiological differences between the sexes. We tend to "process" our interactions with people more than men do; we listen for the unspoken message, consider not just the explicit communication but the more subtle and less easily detected meanings in our relationships and their vicissitudes.

Women value relationships as much as, if not more than, any other aspect of life, which is why it's difficult to distinguish our needs from those of others or decide when to yield our psychological space and when to guard it. We tend to confuse the absence of boundaries with real intimacy, but love that knows no boundaries isn't love at all—it's the fool's gold of relationships, masquerading as that romantic ideal: two hearts beating as one. And even though we may know that control over much of what happens to us is only an illusion, we continue behaving as though it's a reality. And even though we know that love has its limits, we will never stop hoping it doesn't.

That's what the boundaries we're going to consider in these pages are—limits. Necessary, inevitable, and enduring, but also flexible, contextual, and adaptable.

The "Little Black Dress" of Relationships

As a journalist as well as a social psychologist who studies the interpersonal realms of human behavior, I often hear people express their nostalgia for a time when boundaries seemed clearer and more well defined than they are today. All around us the boundaries of society change so rapidly that the definitions of what's public and what's personal, what's right and what's wrong keep changing, too. Is it harassment to tell a woman she has nice legs? Does the public have a right to know about a politician's prescription for Prozac? Is the fictional embellishment of a well-known person's life an invasion of privacy?

A lot of what has been written about boundaries, especially women's boundaries, implies that they're a set of all-purpose standards or rules that fit every situation, with everyone in our lives—like a little black dress that only needs the right accessories to go anywhere. At the heart of this interpretation of boundaries is the assumption that there is one "safe" position on the continuum of relatedness, one that lets enough of our psychological "skin" show without shrouding us in invisibility, that safeguards our integrity and shields us from the danger of letting others get too close to us . . . as if association were the same thing as absorption. We are advised to define, defend, and maintain our boundaries as if they were a Maginot Line that can keep the enemy (other people) from overrunning us.

Several problems arise when looking at boundaries in this way. One is the implied message that women need the protection of boundaries because we are so driven by our nature and our culture to relatedness that the need for boundaries clouds our psychological awareness and limits our capacity to assess a situation, recognize safety or threats relative to our own vulnerability and/or tolerance, and adjust our boundaries accordingly. Another is the mistaken belief that the purpose of all boundaries is to limit rather than expand relatedness—to separate, not connect, us. What comes across in this perspective is the message that allowing someone into our psychological space is an invitation to plunder and destroy it, rather than share or even—gasp!—change it. This is a limited and patronizing view of boundaries. It doesn't include the most important thing about boundaries: that they can be used to connect us to others as well as to separate us from them, on various levels, at different times, according to what we want and need.

This book offers a unique perspective on boundaries—that they are how we connect as well as how we separate, how we invite others in to share our deepest selves as well as how we protect our autonomy and independence from their unwitting or even intentional intrusion. Experiencing our relationships as an expression of boundaries (ours and other people's) can dramatically change the way we meet, know, and engage with the world—personally, emotionally, professionally, and socially. It can strengthen a good relationship, repair a damaged one, and clarify an ambiguous one. What that requires is the cultivation of a unique and particular capacity called *boundary intelligence*, which is the active and purposeful management of the three different dimensions or properties of boundaries—their permeability (how thick or thin they are), their flexibility (how variable they are), and their complexity (how intricate and interconnected they are).

Boundary intelligence exists, at least in its rudimentary form, in everyone, although it's not an ability that's usually acknowledged, like a talent for music or math or complex problem solving. But when it's consciously mastered and developed, it can make you a more loving mate, a wiser parent or adult child, a better friend, and a more balanced, productive, and successful manager of every relationship in your life.

The Four Elements of Boundary Intelligence

Awareness is the first element of boundary intelligence; we can only manage our boundaries if we recognize that a boundary issue—ours or someone else's—has been activated in the relationship. *Insight* is the second—the recognition that we need to adjust the permeability of the boundary between ourself and another person or between our thoughts, feelings, impulses, and fantasies. *Intention*, the third element, is the clarification of a strategy to achieve that objective. *Action*, the fourth element, is the mobilization of any or all the dimensions of boundaries required to put that strategy into action.

Intelligence is the power of mind—boundary intelligence is the power of mind and emotion combined, and the management of both to accommodate two seemingly irreconcilable psychological needs that exist in us and in all our relationships. Boundary intelligence allows us to deepen the quality and meaning of all our relationships without jeopardizing our own autonomy and integrity or sacrificing anyone else's. It allows us to define the limits within which we feel secure, unafraid of being so engulfed by others' needs, whims, and wishes that we lose sight of who we are and what we need. Boundary intelligence helps us understand where, when, and why we draw the line between our true self and the person others expect us to be—our lovers, partners, family, friends, children, colleagues, and casual acquaintances—which frees us to be more real, more ourselves, with everyone in our life.

Boundary Style—Who We Are in All Our Relationships

We all have a characteristic way of relating to others and to ourselves—a boundary style. Boundary style isn't necessarily determined by personality, but it's an aspect of it that influences whether we're fearful or outgoing, spontaneous or controlled, rigid or flexible, demanding or conciliatory, open or closed off. It's what results from the interplay of the three different dimensions of boundaries, determining our level of comfort and safety in every interpersonal situation and influencing how we meet our own needs for distance and closeness in our relationships with others.

Boundaries are dynamic and fluid. As the psychologist Nancy Popp describes, *"Boundary* is a verb as well as a noun." Boundary style is the combination of both those aspects that are expressed in our relationships—including the one we have with our deepest self. When we know and understand our boundary style, we can recognize and respect others's. We can see how different boundary styles—or even the same ones—affect our most important relationships. We can recognize when we need to vary or adapt our boundary style to tone down tension or conflict, increase intimacy and connection, and protect and nurture the self.

Boundary differences are often the cause of friction, discontent, or problems in relationships, although they often masquerade as something else—fights over money, the kids, the in-laws, the deadline, the broken promise, or the forgotten occasion. But understanding how our boundary style and someone else's interact multiplies our options for resolving conflict; reframing the conflict as a boundary issue presents other possibilities for resolution besides giving in or giving up. From a boundary perspective, it's not about who wins and who loses, but about how people negotiate the tangled lines between each other.

You Don't Need to Go Backward to Go Forward

Neither boundaries nor boundary styles are fixed in concrete. They can be modified and even changed without endless and expensive hours on a therapist's couch, a complete psychological makeover, or a sacrifice of your own independence and authenticity. Your constitutional endowment—the nature of your neurology—as well as your own personal, relational history influences your boundary style. But although the boundaries created early in life are always reflected in subsequent relationships, it's not necessary to rehash every moment of your past to change your present. You can start right now, and this book will show you how.

How to Use This Book

While psychological theory and research informs this book, so do the stories, anecdotes, examples, and illustrations drawn from the recognizable, everyday experiences of many people who shared their lives with me. The first chapter provides a basic description of boundaries—what they are, what they do, and how they shape both inner and interpersonal life. The next one explains emotional trespass, which is what happens when boundaries are ignored or violated—something that occurs countless times a day in the give and take of life with other people. Emotional trespass is the chief culprit in many relationships, and as we shall see, it's much easier to recognize it when you're on the receiving end than when you're the one committing it.

Some people are more vulnerable to emotional trespass than others—their boundaries are more permeable, so they feel it more sharply, or less flexible, so they can't protect themselves from it, or not complex enough to enable them to regulate closeness and distance in their relationships without committing emotional trespass themselves. Boundary style determines how you deal with emotional trespass and also how your boundaries satisfy (or don't satisfy) your deepest emotional needs.

The Boundary Style Questionnaire, a five-part self-assessment tool in chapter 3, is the key to identifying your boundary style and mapping the differences in your inner, intimate, and interpersonal boundaries. Like all the shorter quizzes in the succeeding chapters, the questions are as important as the answers; they are designed to hone your boundary awareness, just as the subsequent chapters provide insight about where your boundaries came from, clarification about how they're manifested in your relational life, and strategies for managing them more effectively.

Boundary style isn't as fixed and immutable as the color of your eyes, your right- or left-handedness, or even your IQ. It's not necessarily a given that you'll always have boundary issues with the people you love the most. But understanding your own boundary style allows you to heed or ignore the emotional signals that you get or send when you or someone else comes too close or goes too far away and to manage conflict to achieve both the closeness you crave and the autonomy you need.

A New Way to Strengthen the Relationships That Really Matter

The more prescriptive sections of this book are based not only on psychological theory and research but also on clinical and anecdotal material derived from a number of sources, including the many people who helped me create the Boundary Style Questionnaire and used it to determine their individual boundary style. Their stories—and those of their lovers, spouses, parents, children, significant others, casual friends, colleagues, and coworkers—illustrate how and why boundary intelligence offers a new and different way to manage yourself in your personal and professional relationships rather than letting them manage you.

Once you know where and when you draw your own lines, you'll be more able and willing to respect other people's boundaries instead of trying to erase them. You'll be able to look at difficulties between you and others from a perspective that not only acknowledges but also celebrates your differences. To see conflict as a way to transform your relationships, not just in the moment but over the long haul. Boundary awareness will help you give up insisting on the rightness of your stance or the wrongness of others, and to suggest by example—without saying a word—that others, too, can be flexible enough to find that space between the lines where you can meet, know, and love one another without losing yourself in the process.

Is This Book for You?

Do you sometimes have trouble separating your thoughts, feelings, and judgments from those of others? Are you unsure of the difference between intimacy and merger, invitation and trespass? Do you often feel that other people are crossing your lines or worry that you're crossing theirs? Are you seeking to negotiate the limits of love, balance your work with your life, let your children separate and grow into whole people who still love and respect you? Do you wish you could clean up your troubled relationships, deepen the friendships that really matter, and find a better way to handle stress, conflict, loneliness, and anxiety?

As Carl Jung wrote, "In the deepest sense we all dream not of ourselves, but of what lies between us and the other." This book is about that uncharted territory and the lines that define it.

CHAPTER 1

Boundary Basics: A Primer

Remember the *Seinfeld* episode about the "close talker" who got right in people's faces without noticing how uncomfortable he made them? He had no sense of their spatial boundaries and seemed to have none of his own. Spatial boundaries define the invisible bubble around the body anthropologists call proxemics, or the distance people keep from one another. Proxemics has found that personal space varies not only from person to person but also according to context and culture; what's too close for comfort in Tokyo may be a nodding acquaintance in Naples, while the right amount of space between two people at an American cocktail party might be inappropriate at a business meeting. Even when we have limited control over our physical distance from others—jammed up against a stranger in the subway, for instance, or as far away as we can get from that person on the other side of the bed who's suddenly become one—we can communicate our other external boundaries not only with our overall body language but also by the quality of our attention and the directness of our gaze; our gestures, actions, and expressions of emotion; and our words—all the interpersonal processes of relationship.

Boundaries define what goes on in our minds as well as in the psychological space between us and other people, which is why they are the single most important influence on all our relationships—including the one we have with ourselves. Here is a basic primer that outlines what you need to know about boundaries in order to start managing yours.

Boundaries in the Mind, Boundaries in the World

While boundaries are primarily psychological phenomena, a lot of what we know about the brain suggests that inner (also known as intrapsychic) boundaries may have biological correlates: several theories of the mind based on neuroscience as well as observational evidence point in that direction.

Many theories imply the existence of some type of cellular boundaries between regions of the brain. The triune brain theory, which has been around since 1952 and was first put forth by the evolutionary biologist Paul MacLean at the Laboratory of Brain Evolution and Behavior at the National Institute of Mental Health, distinguishes between the reptilian, limbic, and neocortical brains, in ascending order of evolutionary development, differentiation, and complexity. The reptilian brain, which regulates life itself by managing brain, lung, and heart functions, is concerned with fundamental needs like survival, dominance, preening, hoarding, and mating. While the limbic brain generates and archives emotions, the neocortex with its two cerebral hemispheres controls logic, language, creativity, and thought. Melanie, who is about to turn forty and never wanted a baby until recently, swears it's a signal from her reptilian brain, since she's certainly not in love (a condition generated by the limbic brain) and knows that having a child at this stage of her life and career makes no sense at all (something her neocortex is quite certain about).

Twenty years after MacLean put forth his theory, Roger Sperry at the University of California proposed the left brain/right brain model, which further refined the workings of the cerebral cortex, whose lateral lobes function differently from each other although both sides of the brain are involved in every human activity. According to Sperry's model, one side of the brain processes words while the other handles images; one gets the details accurately while the other sees the whole picture; one analyzes information in a linear, sequential manner while the other absorbs and synthesizes it all, including sensory data. While most people have a distinct preference for one of these styles of knowing, some are more "whole brained" than others and are equally adept at both modes. This model explains why a meal with Kate, who's a left-brained luncher, involves a painstaking analysis of the entrée's ingredients, a thoughtful allocation of the day's calories, and a consideration of what she plans to eat for dinner, while dinner with Peggy, who's as methodical and analytical as Kate but more in touch with her inner sensualist, is punctuated by deep sighs of pleasure and an almost erotic appreciation of the meal's taste, texture, and presentation.

A decade after Sperry, the cognitive psychologist Howard Gardner proposed a theory of multiple intelligences, a label he gave to what most of us knew already, which is that while many people are quite smart in some ways, in certain others they may be less than brilliant. Along with verbal, mathematical, spatial, kinesthetic, and musical intelligences, Gardner identified two other kinds of competencies: intrapersonal intelligence, which is the ability to recognize, manage, and master one's own emotions as they're happening, and interpersonal intelligence, which is the same constellation of skills but involving the emotions of others. These kinds of abilities don't necessarily go together. Lila, who rarely takes her own emotional temperature, isn't particularly self-aware, although she's very responsive to her friends' and colleagues' moods and emotions, while Cecily, who's quite tuned into and sensitive about her own feelings, has little understanding and even less interest in anyone else's.

Boundary intelligence, though, is a meta-ability comprising two different ways of knowing, the rational and emotional, and is expressed not just in thinking and feeling but also in relating; it is intrapsychic and also interpersonal.

Almost everyone has at least a modicum of boundary intelligence; we generally know where we end and others begin, both physically and psychologically. Our bodies are distinct from theirs, and so, most of the time, are our thoughts, emotions, fantasies, and impulses, which have their own unique, distinct mental "signature" because they're internally generated. But what we're largely unaware of is how the contents of our own minds are influenced, changed, or rearranged by those of others, and vice versa. While keeping an open mind is essential for growth and learning, so is being able to discriminate the good from the bad, the wise from the stupid, the truth from the lie, the constructive from the destructive, and especially the toxic from the healthy.

When she was a teenager, Hallie took up with Chloe, who'd recently moved onto her block. Within a month Hallie was "totally under her sway," as she puts it now. "It was like, everything I believed was wrong; suddenly my old friends seemed like losers, doing well in school was a waste of time, obeying my parents was juvenile, being considerate of other people was being a patsy, wanting to be a cheerleader was ridiculous, while shop-lifting, cutting school, and sneaking out of the house to go joy-riding with some kids who'd 'borrowed' a car were the things to do. In a matter of weeks, I'd totally lost sight of who I was; I com-pletely changed myself into a clone of Chloe. Have you seen that movie *Thirteen*? Well, that was me; that was my life after I met Chloe."

When Chloe lost interest in Hallie, Hallie was devastated. "I saw myself through Chloe's eyes—this naive, stupid, ugly girl who couldn't think for herself. And she was right about that last thing— I couldn't, which is probably why I was so vulnerable to her. I'd alienated all my other friends, I was close to flunking out, my parents were at their wits' end, and I had a reputation as a slut so nobody decent would date me."

Lonely, miserable, and friendless, Hallie spent the next few years looking for someone to fill Chloe's place in her life. She found it at a coffee shop frequented by a group of attractive young men and women who sensed her vulnerability and took advantage of it, recruiting her into a cult—the Moonies—that for a while provided a sense of belonging, a code of conduct, and a regimen that almost succeeded in obliterating the last vestiges of her own thoughts, beliefs, and values. "Then one night a new girl came to dinner. She'd been recruited by the same couple who picked me up at the coffee shop almost a year before," Hallie remembers. "I watched how they indoctrinated her—first bombarding her with all this love, and then convincing her that they were the only people who really under- stood her, the same way they had with me. It was like déjà vu—she was me; she even looked like me! I wanted to scream at them to stop, to leave her alone, and tell her to get up and walk out. But I didn't. Instead, I left myself—that very same night, without telling anyone. And for weeks after, I'd see that girl in my dreams. I still wonder what happened to her."

Hallie wasn't ready to return home: "I felt like I'd burned my bridges, and I wouldn't go back until I'd made something of myself." She found a job at a shelter for abused women: "I hadn't been physically abused by a husband the way they had, but I could relate to many of their feelings. I went to the group meetings the res- idents had and listened to their stories, and somehow their courage gave me enough to turn my life around. To this day, whenever someone tells me they know what's best for me, or they know what I'm thinking or feeling, or what I want or need, I pull back from them until I'm sure whose voice I'm really hearing. I've gotten pretty good at keeping the bad stuff out . . . but I'm still working on letting the good stuff in." That's a pretty good description of what psychological boundaries do, and Hallie's increasing ability to use both her cognitive abilities and her emotional awareness to hear, heed, and protect her true self from the psychological influence of others—even well-meaning others—is what boundary intelligence is all about.

The Serpent Made Me Do It, but My Amygdala Was Sorry

If Freud, who was trained as a neurologist in the nineteenth century, had ever seen twenty-first-century neuroscientists actually scanning and mapping the brain and its neural circuitry, he'd have jumped up and shouted "Eureka!" (or its Viennese equivalent). Then he would have located the id, "that cauldron full of seething excitation," as he put it, in the amygdala, an almond-shaped cluster of interconnected cells in the limbic ring where emotions are generated and stored.

The amygdala scans incoming sensory data, "challenging every situation, every perception, with . . . the most primitive question: Is this something I hate? That hurts me? Something I fear?" as the author Daniel Goleman writes in his lucid description of the emotional brain. When aroused, the amygdala floods the entire body with neurochemical signals that leave behind a vivid and indelible trace of fear, anger, grief, happiness, surprise, or shame—whatever feeling triggered it.

The amygdala stores not only the feeling but also the context and meaning provided by the hippocampus, another limbic structure: recounting his conversation with the pioneering neuroscientist Joseph LeDoux, Goleman writes, "As he [LeDoux] put it to me, 'The hippocampus is crucial in recognizing a face as that of your cousin. But it is the amygdala that adds you don't really like her." And all this activity occurs in the limbic system a kazillionth of a second before the neocortex wakes up, smells the coffee, analyzes the feeling, and initiates a more nuanced reaction.

It's in the intricate neural circuitry between the emotional and the rational brains—the limbic ring and the neocortex—that impulses meet reason, feelings and thoughts connect, fantasy and reality collide, and split-off. Repressed, or disavowed aspects of the self drift in and out of the unconscious, which hovers in the hidden corners of the mind, sometimes breaking through into awareness and other times making its presence known in dreams, symbols, enactments, or projections. The thinner or more permeable the boundaries between these mental states are, the more accessible they are to one another. That's why in some particularly emotional situations we literally can't think straight; a powerful surge of feeling hijacks the rational mind, so the more carefully calibrated response from the neocortex barely registers. This will come as no surprise to anyone who's ever fallen in love at first sight, tried to focus on an intellectual task while in the throes of depression, or blown up in anger for what seems like no reason at all.

What Inner Boundaries Do, and Why They Do It

Inner boundaries are shaped by genetic inheritance (individual neurochemistry, the sensitivity of the amygdala, and the connections between various parts of the brain, among other things); our psychic adaptation very early in life to the loss of that common skin the French psychoanalyst Didier Anzieu calls the *moi-peau*, or ego-skin, between mother and baby; and the effect of early environment on psychological as well as physical development.

Temperament, neurochemistry, and habits of mind determine the extent to which our inner boundaries connect or separate our thoughts and feelings, distinguish our mental experiences from those of other people, and absorb or deflect the influence of their thoughts, moods, and voices on our own. They also distinguish among the three aspects of the mind Freud called the id, the ego, and the superego: the id represents all of our instincts, unregulated by conscience or judgment, which are the province of the superego, and unfettered by the ego, which is the conviction of selfhood.

Inner boundaries give our various states of awareness—the conscious, unconscious, and preconscious contents of our minds—their distinct properties. According to Dr. Ernest Hartmann, whose pioneering work on nightmare sufferers led to his conception of boundaries as an aspect of personality, inner boundaries separate the contents of different states of consciousness, each of which has its own characteristic mode of functioning. In the unconscious or dream state, logical connections are missing, contradictions abound, time seems not to exist, nothing is prohibited, and one idea or image can symbolize or condense others. But in normal waking consciousness, these dreams and fantasies are inhibited; the mind is aware of both external events and inner or mental phenomena and is governed by the reality principle, which is represented by logical thought in verbal language form.

When, How, and Why Inner Boundaries Change

Inner boundaries change not only from sleeping to waking states but also as a result of life experiences as varied as falling in love, in which we project our inner fantasies on an external reality and view them both as the same thing (which is why love can often be both blind and dumb), and having a baby, which women often describe as opening a door in their hearts they never knew was there. The psychiatrist Donald Winnicott, in less poetic terms, calls this a "special psychiatric condition of the mother," a state of primary maternal preoccupation characterized by profound attachment and identification with her baby. This merged state is that primal union from which the infant eventually emerges as his or her own mental boundaries develop. Winnicott calls it a "normal sickness" from which mothers recover a few months after giving birth.

Inner boundaries tend to thicken with age as we lose some of the spontaneity, imagination, playfulness, and creativity of early life; while thin inner boundaries allow greater sensitivity to emotional experiences and access to states of awareness such as inspiration and intuition, thicker ones enable us to focus our attention, marshal our thoughts, mobilize our emotions in pursuit of desired goals, make and keep commitments, abide by social rules, deal more productively with stress, and make decisions based more on logic than on gut feelings.

Inner boundaries also change, at least temporarily, when people feel connected to a divine presence—to God, nature, the creative spirit, or what Jung called the collective unconscious. It's what happens to Frances when she's having a particularly good day at her easel: "I feel taken over by this force; it feels like someone or something else is mixing my palette, guiding my brush strokes, as if it knows what a stray thought or a concept or an image ought to look like and is trying to tell me just to let it happen. Sometimes I don't even know what my paintings mean until much later; I sort of sink into them and then feel the presence of that same force again." For Nancy, being in her beloved mountains often engenders a similar feeling: "It's more spiritual than I've ever felt in church—like I'm one with this supreme being who created everyone and everything."

These are often considered right-brain experiences, although regardless of where they actually occur, they may have a more enduring effect on inner boundaries once the brain's entire mental apparatus has analyzed, interpreted, and contextualized them. That's what turns instances of spiritual transcendence into an abiding faith, existential loneliness into a sense of connection with the universe, and flashes of inspiration into works of art. Certain drugs also alter inner boundaries, not only the psychopharmaceuticals used in the treatment of mental illnesses but other substances, legal and illegal, that change the brain's chemistry and promote or inhibit its effects on neuronal activity. Peyote and mescaline have long been used in religious ceremonies to invoke the holy spirit, and hallucinogens such as LSD are used to open what the novelist Aldous Huxley called the "doors of perception." And rituals like chanting and drumming, meant to heighten sensitivity to spiritual experiences, have been associated with increased neurological activity between various regions of the brain. Sue, who's been participating in a women's drumming group for years, likens the experience to "opening up another channel through which the whole world enters my being."

Trauma, fear, loss, or even repeated experiences of emotional trespass may thicken inner boundaries in order to wall feelings off from thoughts, split off unacceptable emotions from consciousness, repress painful memories by keeping them out of awareness, or deny a reality that's too difficult to accept. These psychological defenses are not themselves boundaries—they are the means by which inner boundaries are maintained.

Is That a Cell Phone in Your Pocket, or Are You Hearing Voices?

Inner boundaries serve many important functions. They protect us from the primitive agonies of going to pieces, falling forever, and having no relation to our bodies and no orientation in time or space. They separate the parts of us we can accept from those that are too shameful or scary to bring to awareness. A person with faulty or missing inner boundaries can't tell the difference between what's inside himself and what's outside. He has no protection against his own or even other people's thoughts, fears, and fantasies, no control over sensory input, and no grounding in reality. Conversely, someone whose inner boundaries are so fixed, rigid, and impenetrable that his body, mind, and emotions are inaccessible to one another can't take in anything at all and may suffer from a mental illness on the obsessive-compulsive continuum: mild to severe autism or even catatonia.

In much of the psychiatric literature, firm, thick intrapsychic boundaries are considered healthy and adaptive. They have been associated with a strong superego or conscience; a memory bank with an excellent "retrieval system" that gets from the past only what's necessary to deal with the present and the future; and a sense of personal identity that is firm and constant rather than flexible or situational. By contrast, thin, permeable inner boundaries are often viewed as weak or defective. Those judgments, however, reflect both a clinical population of severely disturbed individuals and the gender bias that stems from the finding that overall, women have thinner boundaries, and norms and standards of psychological development have traditionally been based on male models.

The Meaning of What Happens

When inner boundaries are doing what they're supposed to do, they make it possible for us to relate to our inner world rather than being taken over by it. If that's confusing, think of a two-year-old in a high chair. You can almost see it happening an instant before he tosses his Cheerios happily on the floor; at two, he doesn't *have* that impulse, he *is* it. If it's been awhile since you were around a two-year-old, remember the intensity of your first love affair: you didn't *have* that romance, you *were* it. And you had as much trouble managing your moods and emotions as that two-year-old because, like him, you weren't in control, your feelings were.

Inner boundary structure is the single most important influence on boundary style because it reflects the mind's ongoing process of meaning making, which is not just thinking about an experience but organizing it—perceiving, selecting, interpreting, labeling, and classifying it. We organize our thoughts, feelings, beliefs, fantasies, and associations according to principles that become increasingly more complex as our minds mature. But the most elemental meaning we assign to our mental experience is not whether it's good or bad, true or false, logical or irrational, but whether it belongs in and to the self; as the Harvard psychologist Robert Kegan writes, whether we *are* it or *have* it—whether it feels inside or outside, whether we're embedded in it or can relate to it. This distinction, or boundary, between self and other, subject and object, Me and Not Me, is always in flux. It's always evolving, in a process we call psychological individuation and Buddhist philosophers express as a movement toward higher consciousness; the capacity to relate to what we were previously attached to or embedded in, a capacity that the two-year-old who's a creature of his impulses hasn't yet developed, or that someone whose emotional brain has been hijacked by love won't be able to exercise until after the rapture fades.

The Connection between Inner Boundaries and Addiction

Much of what has been said and written about boundaries derives from the recovery movement, which isn't surprising, since boundary distortion, dysfunction, and confusion are symptomatic of problems with drugs, alcohol, food, sex, spending, and other substances and activities that are, or are considered to be, addictions. But while the addiction and recovery literature touches on boundaries, generally it gives short shrift to inner boundaries and focuses instead on interpersonal ones—not necessarily the addict's, but those of his or her "enablers" or "codependents," people whose even well-meaning attempts at helping the addict often make the addict's problems—and problem behaviors—worse.

As Allie, a twelve-stepper in recovery for a ten-year alcohol problem, says, "They don't tell you that trying to understand why you drink is unimportant, but they're pretty dismissive about the psychology of it—they think all you need to do is admit you don't have control over the drug and turn your will over to your higher power and work the steps; that's what it's all about, everything else is denial or justification. The issues that underlie the addiction—like the need to stay in an abusive relationship, which have a lot to do with mine—they don't come in for much examination."

In the psychiatric literature, addiction is a disorder of self-regulation, particularly in the areas of emotion, self-care, self-esteem, and relationships, although some theorists view it as an attachment disorder, which offers insight into why some vulnerable people need to substitute chemical connections or solutions for human ones. Clinical approaches based on this view of addiction focus on interpersonal as well as inner boundaries.

Is It a Symptom or a Disease?

Addiction is a dependency on something that stimulates, suppresses, erases, or substitutes for whatever is unwanted or missing in our inner or interpersonal lives: control, rage, emptiness, shame, boredom, drama, power, love, panic, or perfection, for example. Addiction may be a neurotic stand-in for legitimate suffering or emotional pain, desperate mental states for which the desired process (as in eating disorders, sexual compulsivity, overspending, even exercise) or substance (alcohol, drugs, food) holds out the promise of fulfillment or release.

Most approaches to treating addictions ignore the consideration of inner boundaries; they focus on behavioral therapies that prevent relapse, offer strategies for coping with cravings, and teach addicts ways to avoid drugs, alcohol, and what Allie calls "occasions of sin." These approaches are often directly related to recovery and rarely to the root cause. Addictions can take many forms, and the line between acceptable and problem behaviors isn't always clear. But the one definite, even simplistic indicator of an addiction is that the addict keeps going back to whatever the substance or the behavior is, even though he doesn't want to do it again, or when even more copious amounts of whatever he craves don't satisfy the craving.

The boundaries of addiction are constantly redrawn in our culture, as a variety of types of self-destructive behavior are relabeled
as addictive; many professionals concur that it's the strength of the
desire that defines addiction. Judy, who lives to shop, has enough
self-control to avoid a 50 percent off sale at Loehmann's when her
credit cards are maxed out, but that wouldn't stop Elaine, who
doesn't, despite lawsuits, bankruptcies, and the loss of her house
and her car. Judy's addiction to cigarettes, though, is another matter—she's tried and failed to quit so many times that this January
her New Year's resolution is to stop trying.

Simple addiction is superficial dependence that involves physical craving and withdrawal symptoms when the substance is
removed. In many cases it can be modified without in-depth
approaches like psychotherapy or twelve-step or professional reha-
bilitation programs. It's reversible by means of willpower and individual effort. Simple addiction touches only a part of the addict's
personality; another, sometimes larger part, either opposes the
addiction, fights it and overcomes it, or makes it worse by building
it up. That's how Judy curbed her shopping compulsion; she cut up
her credit cards, made a budget and stuck to it, and gave herself a
reward every time she went into a store and came out empty-
handed (unfortunately, her customary reward was a cigarette). For
her, smoking has a psychological hold on her that's much more
powerful than physical need, which is why even when she's managed to stay off cigarettes for months at a time, she's always
relapsed. Willpower and simple habit-breaking techniques that
were so successful in reining in her shopping habit and sticking to
a diet long enough to lose twenty pounds (and keep them off) don't
work.

Inner boundaries are the source of addiction. If they're too rigid,
we're unable to connect deeply enough with our emotions to har-
ness them in the service of our cognitive process or use our cogni-
tions—like the knowledge that the substance or the behavior is
self-destructive—to control our impulses. If they're too permeable,

we can't discern the differences between our feelings, sensations, and impulses. We don't *have* them, we *are* them, and they're easily influenced by external as well as internal forces—peer pressure, social conditioning, and the behavior of others.

Mental Health or Mental Growth?

Research has shown that boundaries and boundary style influence not only our relationships with other people but also our emotional balance; personal values; cognitive abilities; career choice; preferences in art, architecture, and music; political views and opinions; and attitudes toward time and money! Given how important boundaries are in so many areas of life, it's surprising how often they're overlooked as an influence on personality, especially by psychiatrists and psychologists whose primary focus is on the individual rather than on the individual-in-relation. They're more concerned with inner boundaries than interpersonal ones because distorted or dysfunctional inner boundaries are often a hallmark of mental illness. Even if our inner boundaries aren't so distorted that we're curled up in a corner of a padded room or hearing voices when nobody's calling, most clinical psychologists and psychiatrists are more interested in our mental health than in our psychological growth.

Interpersonal psychologists think about inner boundaries differently; they focus on how inner boundaries shape our social relationships as well as how they organize (or don't organize) the contents of our minds. Interpersonal psychologists know that when inner boundaries are too weak or too porous, the self is empty and famished, forever in search of someone or something to fill it up; when they are too solid and rigid, the self can never be known, touched, or moved. And when inner boundaries are distorted, so is the possibility of psychological growth.

Boundary intelligence involves the understanding and mastery of inner as well as interpersonal boundaries. Boundary style, though, depends on the particular qualities or dimensions of those boundaries themselves.

The Dimensions of Boundaries

What does the wind do when it's not blowing? What happens to noise when it's being quiet? What does tofu taste like when it doesn't taste like something else? And why can't I have another cookie?

The only one of six-year-old Noah's questions I can answer is the last one, and so great is my relief that I indulge a grandmother's prerogative and give him one. I consider that what his mother calls her son's Zen koans are not just riddles wrapped in paradoxes, they're Noah's attempts at organizing the phenomena of his experience into a mental set or class with its own properties—what Robert Kegan calls "durable categories"—in much the same way that he used to organize his toys into things with wheels and things without wheels. What Noah wants to know is what else wind, sound, and tofu *are* besides how he perceives them—how they feel, sound, and taste to him.

What else are boundaries besides how we experience them in relationships? What qualities, dimensions, and tendencies do they have in addition to their affective, intrapersonal, and interpersonal properties? What makes them a noun as well as a verb?

As we've seen, psychological boundaries are dynamic, not static. They change not only from one relationship to another but also within relationships, in a back-and-forth, interactional process set in motion not just by what's going on within each person but also according to what's happening between them at any given time. What boundaries do is differentiate one thing or one self from another, thus setting the two things or selves in some relation to each other.

The Soluble Self

Boundaries have certain inherent qualities and dimensions, chiefly permeability, complexity, and flexibility. The first of these, permeability, seems to be a relatively stable aspect of personality—how penetrable we generally are to the psychological influence of the thoughts, feelings, judgments, and affects of others. What the psychiatrist Louis Ormond called a healthy "insulation barrier" is a boundary structure that's permeable enough to allow experience to penetrate the inner self but solid enough to protect it from being overcome by internal impulses and external demands or overwhelmed by toxic stimuli like critical or negative judgments, ideas, views, and emotions, our own as well as other people's.

High inner permeability means that there's more connection than separation in our mind between and among its discrete parts; our thoughts and feelings run together, our moods shift easily, our views and opinions fluctuate. Interpersonally, too, increased permeability usually implies more connection than separation, although that doesn't necessarily mean we're always able to discriminate the good from the bad, to take in the positive, nourishing, affirming input from others and keep out what might be critical, negative, or damaging. The permeability of our inner boundaries determines how much we can absorb of what comes in from the outside without losing what makes us distinctly ourselves; how free the energy flow is between us; the exchange of affect, emotion, and ideas; our ability to screen out others' influence and separate our sense of self from their psychological presence within us; and how much we use other people to constitute who we are.

High permeability permits a relatively free flow of energy between inside and outside, self and others. Since childhood, Caroline's parents, teachers, and friends have described her as sensitive, vulnerable, imaginative, and restless; in fact, those are the words under her portrait in her senior yearbook. She's very approachable but also so gullible that she's an easy mark for beggars and con artists; highly receptive to outside stimuli, she's easily distracted from her goal or purpose. By contrast, Elizabeth's less permeable boundaries constrain the energy flowing between inside and outside, but they also make it easier for her to focus on the task at hand. She's often unaware of her inner experience and less available to her imagination and creativity than Caroline, but she's also less impressionable or as likely to take on the moods and feelings of others. More fixed in her judgments and beliefs and more direct and explicit in her thinking than Caroline, Elizabeth's also more capable of masking her emotions and repressing painful feelings as well as better able to balance outside demands on her time and energy.

Fences of Chicken Wire, Wooden Slats, and Concrete

Nancy Popp, whose exploration of the phenomenon of boundaries provides the description of them as both a noun and a verb (and whose conception of them inspired this book, especially this chapter), offers a metaphor that likens boundaries to fence-building materials—her examples are chicken wire, wooden slats, and concrete. Chicken wire is the most permeable; it allows a lot to pass through, and although chicken wire provides little protection from external forces or the escape of big chunks of the self, it still manages to contain it. The wooden slat fence lets fewer and smaller bits of the self and others in and out; it provides more separation and protection. Concrete lets nothing pass through from either side and requires a very conscious decision to allow it to be crossed in either direction.

All or Nothing at All

Boundary complexity is determined more by one's stage of psychological development than by personality, and it tends to increase as we move from one level of psychological growth to the next. Complexity refers to the increasing ability to differentiate, and thus relate to, the various parts or aspects of the self—its roles, identities, actions, emotions, sensations, and associations—without losing a coherent sense of the whole—of who the self is. In other words, complexity is about being able to see the trees and the forest simultaneously, the parts and the system, the contents of the mind and the container that holds them. When Noah was three and threw sand in a playmate's face because she wouldn't give him back his red plastic pail, he couldn't quite get the distinction his mother made between him and his behavior. "I love you, but I don't like the way you're acting," she'd say, but as far as he was concerned, who he was and what he did were the same thing.

Boundary complexity explains why, for instance, we can admire a friend's intellectual gifts, enjoy her sense of humor, and appreciate her generosity even though we don't share or care for other aspects of her, like her political or sexual values or her inability to keep a secret. "Sometimes the reception's only clear on one or two channels, but that doesn't mean you have to throw the TV set away," explains Petra, who is able to tolerate competing emotions, loyalties, priorities, and desires in herself without coming apart at the seams, just as she can separate from as well as connect with a number of people in her life who are very different from her. This means she can often find at least one aspect of someone in order to make a relationship possible (which explains how she can sleep with a man she wouldn't want to wake up with).

The more complex our boundaries are, the more parts of our self we can bring to a relationship and the greater the possibilities are for feeling understood and accepted in at least some of those aspects. Since the more of the self we expose, the more vulnerable we are, we may be less willing to be seen or known in our entirety by someone else. And even though we're safer, we're also more separate and disconnected from our authentic self, too. Often we hold back what we feel the least confident about, especially with people whose expectations, opinions, perceptions, and experiences of us constitute a big chunk of our self-definition. Jeanette, who never went to college and is married to a man with three advanced degrees, feels the least confident about her intellectual ability; Ellen, who's always been self-conscious about her body, is disconnected from her sexuality; Trina, who was raised by a couple of doctors who didn't believe in anything they couldn't see under a microscope or grow in a petri dish, is cut off from her emotions.

When the complexity of our boundaries is limited, we can't tolerate too many differences between ourselves and other people and still feel whole. Our feelings, ideas, and judgments must match theirs because we're unable to manage ambivalent or opposing ones. We have trouble holding onto our position in a conflict or a confrontation because it seems like a global assault on our very essence—we feel like we're coming apart. One negative comment from someone important to our sense of self-esteem—something that indicates she doesn't know, accept, or "get" us in a significant way—can make us feel totally rejected; not just that aspect of ourselves but all of us. But when we can tolerate or contain our differences without losing track of or contact with the rest of who we (and they) are, we can be connected to as well as separate from others in more than one way; there are more possibilities for relatedness between us. In other words, the more differentiated we are (the more complex our boundaries), the more we can choose what we share and what we hold back.

For some people, differentiation is the same thing as separation. Says a woman quoted in Letty Pogrebin's book on friendship, "I don't make a huge distinction between myself and others so I have very little sense of distance when I meet a new person. No one seems strange to me." But as the following comment indicates, that position also puts her at somewhat of a disadvantage: "I like everyone right away and feel like I'm the one who has something to prove."

Contrast this with Steffie's more complex boundaries: "I used to think everyone was alike—nothing human was alien to me," she says. "So I tended to ignore or discount how different people actually are from each other and from me. But as I've gotten older, the differences interest me more than the similarities. I'm more curious, more open to the unfamiliar, more aware of the incredible variety of people in the world. Instead of thinking, wow, is that person strange, I just think, well, *that* was a *National Geographic* experience!"

Locking the Door vs. Leaving It Open

Flexibility is the capacity to regulate boundary permeability, the range of motion between how open and closed we can be to the psychological surround. Often we exercise this capacity instinctively or intuitively, without really being conscious of it. We tune out what our teenager's saying while he's driving in order to shout, "Look out for that stop sign!" before he runs through it. Or we tell a stranger more about ourself than we ordinarily might because there's something about him that seems to invite such disclosures, or because we know we'll never see him after the plane lands, or because we really need to talk (or because of all of these things).

At other times, we exercise the flexibility of our boundaries with both awareness and choice; we redirect the conversation with our mother-in-law in order to keep it from affecting how we feel about the house we just bought that she doesn't like, or we adjust the volume or intensity of our relationship with a friend or a colleague whose energy, moods, or force of personality overwhelms and exhausts us.

Flexibility, more than either permeability or complexity, depends on the ability to assess a situation or an individual in terms of safety or threat to the self and adjust our boundaries accordingly. It's the extent to which our boundaries can "give" under pressure or stress from inside (what we think, know, and feel about ourselves) or outside (what the situation, person, or environment is telling us).

Looking at boundaries in this multidimensional way lets us see that while being open to other people in all ways, at all times, is a nice idea in theory, in practice it is a very vulnerable stance. Being closed off is much less risky—it reduces the possibility that we'll be psychologically engulfed or annihilated—but it also restricts the possibilities of any connection or relatedness at all. Miranda's boundaries are extremely permeable but hardly flexible at all; she suffers from sensory overload, and other people's unhappiness "cuts through me like a knife, no matter how good a mood I'm in to begin with." Annabel's boundaries are as permeable as Miranda's, but they're much more flexible, which is why she can ignore chatter from her cubicle next to the watercooler, empathize with her coworkers' fears that layoffs are coming, and then get back to her own work without letting their concerns interfere with her concentration.

Managing boundaries isn't possible until we understand them as both a noun and a verb . . . not just their particular qualities or dimensions, but how they determine what happens in our rela-tional life. Just as a dress or a coat can look one way in a magazine or on the hanger and different when we put it on, boundaries can look or feel different according to the circumstance in which they're activated. They may be quite permeable when we're with someone we love and trust, when we're untroubled, even unconsciously, by fears of being swallowed up or abandoned. Boundaries may be less permeable when we're with someone who doesn't respect our limits, or so one-dimensional that we can't relate to those who don't endorse our beliefs or lifestyle. Boundaries might be complex enough to allow us to connect on some level even with people whose values are diametrically opposed to ours, or conversely, to prevent us from connecting at all with people who are very similar to us.

Boundaries manifest themselves in relationships when internal or external signals activate them. Most commonly the signals mean that someone's violated our psychological space, which is the definition of emotional trespass, although in moments of greater closeness or intimacy signals may also indicate that our boundaries are shifting because we've invited someone into that space.

There are four principles of boundary intelligence. *Awareness*, the first principle, is about being alert to those signals. Once you are, you can exercise the second principle, *insight*, which is a cognitive rather than an emotional analysis of what's happening in the moment. The third is *intention*, or clarifying what you want to happen in the relationship over time as well as right now. And the fourth principle, *action*, is about mobilizing and managing your boundaries to bring about what you want to happen. As Rainer Maria Rilke wrote, "Once the realization is accepted that even between the closest human beings infinite distance continues to exist, a wonderful living side by side can grow up if they succeed in loving the distance between them, which makes it possible for each to see the other whole."

CHAPTER 2

Emotional Trespass and Other Crimes of the Heart

In a perfect world, other people would never let us down. They would let us go when it was time to lead our own lives and hold us close when we wanted their embrace. They would support us when we needed to be alone and understand when we didn't take their advice. They would respect our commitments to others and honor our obligations to ourselves. They would keep our secrets, take our side in a dispute with someone else, and if we were wrong, they wouldn't tell us till later.

The people we live with wouldn't borrow our best sweater without asking, put an empty pint of Häagen-Dazs back in the freezer, read our e-mail, leave the door open when they use the toilet, go through our things, agree with our mother-in-law that the kids need more discipline, or make moves on our girlfriends (and if they did, our girlfriends wouldn't tell us even if we asked).

In a perfect world, our bosses would never ask us to do something unethical, sleazy, or illegal, or blame us for someone else's mistakes. They would know the difference between our jobs and our personal lives. Our colleagues would never pass our work off as their own, confuse honest feedback with a personal attack, ask for information they have no right to know, or share private information with others.

They wouldn't sabotage us with our managers or undermine us with our employees, stab us in the back, or set us up to take a fall.

In a perfect world, our friends would never fail us and our families would never disappoint us. Our lovers would never betray us or always expect us to put their needs above our own, and if some of the time we didn't put them first, they wouldn't stop loving us.

But even in a less-than-perfect world, it's possible to balance the desire for freedom with the need for limits, the demands of our lives with those of our jobs, and our cravings for closeness with our need for distance. It's possible to say no without feeling guilty and yes without feeling manipulated; to love other people without losing ourselves; to keep others from trespassing on our feelings and take care not to trespass on theirs.

Emotional trespass is a crime of the heart, which in its maddeningly human way insists on denying the reality that no matter how close we are to another person, how well we know him, how much like us she seems to be, how attuned we are to his needs and desires or her dreams, we can never really know what it feels like to be someone else, and vice versa. Thus we can never know for certain where people's No Trespassing signs are posted, and often they're not sure where ours are, either.

Emotional trespass is a boundary violation—an unasked-for, uninvited intrusion into our own psychological space. As the psychiatrist Leston Havens writes, "Because there are no public trials for psychological trespass, we can only describe suspects, and that chiefly by their effect on us." In other words, we may not know exactly where our boundaries are, but we know when they've been violated. Feelings like anger, betrayal, fear, shame, or powerlessness sound the silent alarm, telling us someone's too close for comfort, taking too many liberties, making the wrong assumptions about us, invading our privacy, or ignoring our limits. Too often we stuff down those feelings, which rarely gets us what we want—acknowledgment, respect, and reassurance that it won't happen again.

We're more sensitive to and aware of our own alarm than other people's, which is why sometimes we don't pick up their signals that warn us we're trespassing. So we're confused and upset when those we love most respond by pushing us away or discouraging our attempts at connection or our desire for intimacy.

Notes from the Women's Locker Room

Here are some examples of emotional trespass that come not from a therapist's case file (although all therapists have heard these or similar tales from their clients) but from the women's locker room at my gym.

"I had to tell her he's seeing someone else, too. It might hurt her now, but it's for her own good."

"He just won't share his feelings, no matter how much I try to get him to open up."

"Every time he has a tough day at work he takes it out on the whole family."

"Whenever we get together, she just unloads all her problems on me . . . sometimes I feel like her personal dump."

"My husband went through my cell phone bill and called every number he didn't recognize and asked them who they were and how they knew me—can you believe it?"

"I've got a right to read my daughter's diary—after all, she still lives under my roof, doesn't she?"

"I saw a bottle of Prozac in her medicine cabinet. I wonder why she didn't tell me she was taking antidepressants. And he's on Viagra, too!"

"My daughter is such a terrible housekeeper—if it wasn't

for me, the board of health would probably close their house down."

"I always pretend to come. If I didn't, he'd think he was a lousy lover. Which he is, by the way, but so what, at least he's straight and single."

"If you really wanted to lose weight, you could. It's probably a matter of low self-esteem. Or maybe you don't really want to be in a relationship, and if you're fat, you won't have one."

As I soak away my postaerobic aches and pains and listen to them talk, I wonder: When perfect strangers tell each other things I'd only confess to my dog or my pillow, is emotional trespass really such a big deal? And can't an otherwise satisfying relationship surmount a few tactless, careless, unimportant transgressions like these?

When Emotional Trespass Isn't Just a Sometime Thing

If relationships couldn't surmount emotional trespass, the divorce rate would be 100 percent instead of hovering around 50 percent, parents and their adult kids would go their own way and never have anything to do with each other, friends would stop being friends, and workers would communicate electronically instead of dealing with their colleagues face-to-face.

Since emotional trespass is usually a relationship misdemeanor, not a felony, most of the time we get over it. We put that boundary violation and the hurt feelings it provokes into our emotional equivalent of the junk drawer. But then it keeps happening until the drawer is overflowing and the love, understanding, and goodwill that characterize our relationship with the trespasser is abraded and worn away. That's when good relationships start to go bad and problematic ones become more trouble than they're worth.

Adding Insight to Injury

As someone who's always trying to figure out why things go sour with my friends or south with my lover, a situation seems beyond my control, the balance between my work and the rest of my life is out of whack, my family disappoints me, the line blurs between fantasy and reality, or my emotional resources just aren't up to the daily challenge of other people, I've come to realize that the concept of emotional trespass often supplies the answer to these and many other vexing questions: Will my mother ever stop trying to run my life? Is it okay for my husband to have a friend of the opposite sex? Can my best friend still be friends with the woman who stole my man? Can I still tell my office pal the watercooler gossip now that she's my manager? Will I ever stop wondering if the people who love me would still love me if they really, really knew me? And will a bowl of noodles ever be just pasta Alfredo instead of a struggle to stay in control?

How you deal with emotional trespass has a lot to do with your boundary permeability. High permeability explains why you feel depressed after hearing a friend who's been miserable since her husband left her recount the whole sorry saga again. Low permeability explains why you shut out your lover and close down just when he's feeling amorous instead of telling him you're worried about your big presentation tomorrow or you're having second thoughts about your relationship. Medium permeability is why you can notice but not fixate on minor instances of emotional trespass, consider the source and the circumstances, and not let it affect you very deeply.

How other people deal with emotional trespass when they're on the receiving end of it reflects their boundary permeability, too. It explains why the daughter who used to tell you everything treats you like a stranger since you told her soccer coach that she had a crush on her. Why that new neighbor went cold on you just as the friendship seemed to be warming up, after you told her you were thinking of getting divorced. Why your mother won't come to the rehearsal dinner unless you invite her sister, who remembers and replays every embarrassing moment of your childhood in front of your friends.

Taking It Personally—Who Doesn't?

In Maggie's family, emotional trespass isn't just an occasional lapse on someone's part; it was all too common in the family she was born into, and it's a habit that's hung on in her second one, too. "My father used to walk around the house naked. My mother told her friends when I first got my period. My sister told our priest about my abortion. Now my husband tells everyone in his carpool when I have PMS. My son told my mother-in-law I didn't really have to go out of town for a conference, I just don't like the way she rearranges all the furniture every time she comes. My parents keep telling me I'm selfish for only wanting one child and warning me that I'll ruin Todd's life if I don't give him a baby brother or sister. My mother actually went into my bureau drawer and threw out my diaphragm the last time she visited. Does everyone live in a fishbowl or is it just me?"

Michelle offers plenty of examples of repeated emotional trespass in her office. "The head of HR told a woman in my department that I put in a claim on my health insurance for my son's drug treatment program and she spread it around by e-mail. My boss calls me at home on weekends for no good reason except she doesn't have any other life except work. My team leader can't stop talking about his sex life. My closest friend at work got promoted over me and now she's always criticizing me."

And here's Cynara, who has just one, not uncommon comment on boundary violations and emotional trespass: "I'm sick and tired of too much information—of knowing too many things about too many people, most of whom I've barely met, not to mention wondering what they know and are saying about me!"

Maybe You're Just Too Sensitive

Few instances of emotional trespass escape Dorrie's notice, and repeat offenders are banished from her life—even when they're relatives. She's a woman of strong opinions, one of them being that Barbie, that icon of feminine stereotypes, will never find a home in hers. (Did I forget to mention that little Morgan, Dorrie's daughter, could say "gender bias" before she could tie her own shoes?) Dorrie overheard her sister telling me at Morgan's sixth birthday party that she wanted to give her niece a Barbie, but Dorrie wouldn't allow it. "Three boundary violations in one!" Dorrie complained later. "The one between you and me, the one between her and me, and the one between Morgan and me! She's never coming to this house again!"

Sometimes what Dorrie experiences as boundary violations don't seem so awful to me. But maybe that's because my own boundary style is much more permeable than hers—and besides, I didn't grow up with four sisters who ransacked my closet, read my diary, and ignored my need for privacy.

Thea would never go through her daughter's drawers, betray her siblings' confidences, take sides in an argument between her kids and her husband, or discuss her sex life with anyone but him. But she has a harder time distinguishing between other peoples' appetites, sensations, and feelings and her own. And while Thea has spent hours in therapy trying not to turn into her mother—a woman who still thinks her adult kids are an extension of her rather than individuals with their own thoughts, emotions, and agendas—she can't break the habit of telling her friends and family when they're hot, cold, full, hungry, tired, cranky, or anxious—which is usually when she is.

Courtney isn't too clear on what a boundary is, but she certainly knows what it costs—the seven hundred dollars she paid H&R Block to do the family's taxes this year instead of turning them over to Charlie, her husband's best friend, who always does them for free. Michael hit the roof when he found out. "He accused me of being a spendthrift," she says. "Whenever we fight, it's always about money." But this wasn't another fight about money—it was about what happened last year, when Charlie shared the details of their 1040 with his wife, who told their mutual friends that Courtney had a face-lift, her son spent two weeks in a mental hospital, and Michael lost a bundle in the stock market. "I don't need a shrink to tell me why I felt violated," she adds. But if she had one—or even if she just read this book—she'd understand that some of the other fights she and Michael have about what seem to be financial issues aren't always or only about money; their basic conflict is between their boundary styles, even though dollars and cents are the ground on which they battle.

While permeability is the aspect of boundary style that has the most to do with whether you suffer—or commit—emotional trespass, flexibility is what enables you to protect yourself against it, and complexity is what gives you more options for dealing with it to strengthen and improve the relationships that mean the most to you and keep the rest in their place—which is just where you want them.

The next chapter quantifies your boundaries by assessing their dimensions with the Boundary Style Questionnaire and analyzing their structure by determining your boundary style. This is important because you can't manage your boundaries until you know where they are.

CHAPTER 3

What's Your Boundary Style?

You can't exercise your boundary intelligence and manage your boundaries until you know what they're like—how permeable, flexible, and complex they are as well as how and why they differ in different relationships. Your boundary style indicates how those three different dimensions of boundaries influence your relationships—how they affect your inner, intimate, and interpersonal life. The Boundary Style Questionnaire is a simple, self-administered fifty-item quiz that may seem similar to personality tests you've taken before, either at school or at work. But it looks at one aspect of personality that most of those tests don't.

What You Can Learn from a Good (or Bad) Night's Sleep

Dreams, said Freud, are the royal road to the unconscious. Researchers since Freud have studied other aspects of dreaming and sleeping and the many states of consciousness in between in which the mind is disconnected from its daily routine of thinking and feeling, sorting and sifting, forgetting and remembering.

One of these researchers, Dr. Ernest Hartmann, noticed that people who reported frequent nightmares shared certain characteristics. They lived somewhat atypical lifestyles—many were in creative rather than blue- or white-collar jobs. They described themselves as unusually sensitive, empathetic, and easily hurt. They struck Hartmann, a psychiatrist by training, as particularly open and often overly trusting. They tended to become involved in relationships quickly and easily, sometimes with painful results. And they seemed to have been open, sensitive, vulnerable, and artistic from early childhood.

In a psychological sense, Hartmann noticed, they also seemed undefended, more so than others who repress, isolate, or intellectualize frightening, unpleasant, inappropriate, or otherwise dangerous thoughts, feelings, and urges. They tended to merge the contents of their minds in the states between waking and sleeping. While as a group they were as mentally healthy, sound, and well functioning as those who either didn't have nightmares or couldn't recall them, they seemed, both asleep and awake, to have thinner boundaries in their minds and also in their relationships in the world.

Hartmann concluded from his research that boundaries represented a neglected dimension of personality, and he hypothesized that boundary structure might be related to many aspects of life. He devised a questionnaire that included many qualities of various boundaries. And, while no questionnaire can reach deep into the unconscious, this instrument provided a new type of mental map, derived from classical psychology, that enabled him to assess where an individual's boundaries tended to cluster on a continuum of permeability from thick to thin. The more a person separated his thoughts from his feelings, for example, the more psychological space he put between himself and others and the thicker (less permeable) his boundaries were, while the less he did so, the more psychologically influenced he tended to be by others and the thinner (more permeable) his boundaries were.

Hartmann's Boundary Questionnaire is comprised of 145 questions that measure twelve different categories of inner and outer boundaries from environmental preferences to habits and opinions related to work and play, group membership, decision making, and how people organize their lives. But among all of these, the particular boundaries that most influence relationships are intrapsychic (within) and interpersonal (between)—those that describe how we organize the contents of our mind and those that describe our social behavior.

Before Hartmann published his groundbreaking findings, boundaries had primarily been assessed by projective tests like the Rorschach or Thematic Apperception test, which require interpretation by qualified investigators, usually psychiatrists, who are primarily looking for evidence of pathology—disturbances in normal mental functioning, such as the inability to distinguish fantasy from reality. On the other hand, personality tests, which are designed to describe or evaluate character, behavior, temperament, and disposition, offer little information about boundaries. These typologies or inventories are used for many different purposes. The Myers-Briggs test, an instrument familiar to those who work for large corporations, classifies people by their similarities and differences in four different dimensions: how they focus their energy, take in information, make decisions, and approach life—that is, whether they prefer structure and defined goals or keeping their options open. Input from these self-administered questionnaires is primarily used to match an individual's specific traits, qualities, and characteristics to appropriate tasks and objectives in the organization. The Birkman inventory, another popular instrument, uses a combination of self-assessment and feedback from coworkers, managers, and subordinates to determine how people work, learn, and react to stress, the better to understand and use an individual's strengths and weaknesses in advancing corporate as well as personal goals.

Items on the Hartmann and other instruments relating to group boundaries, decision making, and preferences in how people organize and prioritize everything from their time to their cubicle have some connection to performance as well as satisfaction in their careers. It's questionable, however, whether the personality tests (especially the Myers-Briggs) that are increasingly being used by professional matchmakers and online dating services (not to mention businesses and media aimed at the singles market) are of as much value in predicting the success of a personal relationship as they are to a business's bottom line. While they may tap into elements that are important for good teamwork, which is certainly part of what makes a couple click, being the same personality type doesn't have much to do with sexual chemistry.

While Hartmann's research was the starting point for the Boundary Style Questionnaire, his instrument measures only one dimension of boundaries—permeability. It doesn't take into account the effect of either complexity or flexibility, which are key to evaluating the capacity for differentiation among and between various aspects of self and nonself—in other words, of Me and Not Me—or enlighten the understanding of how, when, and why boundaries change in certain kinds of relationships. For instance, while a description of Jessica's boundaries as thick wouldn't be surprising in any criminal defense lawyer who's seen enough of the world's seamy side to keep her guard up, it might not also indicate that her last two boyfriends told her she was too "needy," or that she sometimes tells her friends confidential facts about her clients (especially juicy or titillating ones). Describing Dolores's boundaries as thin might explain why even when this talented writer is on deadline, she finds it hard to focus her thoughts, and why one even slightly negative review can bring on a migraine and make her doubt herself not only as a writer but also as a human being. But it wouldn't also explain that her boundaries are so stuck in the "open" position that she can't close them down when she needs to concentrate on her work, or so undifferentiated that she can't distinguish between what she does and who she is.

Is Thinner Always Better?

What does it mean to say your boundaries are relatively thick or impermeable, but your boundary flexibility is high? Or that your boundaries are quite thin but not very flexible? What can scores on a questionnaire tell you about yourself? More important, what can they do for you?

Despite the metaphors from concrete to chicken wire that are often used to describe them, like all psychological constructs, boundaries are an abstraction—a theoretical variable invented to explain experience. This makes measuring or assessing boundaries in any one person, at any specific time or in any particular relationship, both art and science. And it's not necessarily true, as we will see, that thin boundaries are better than thick ones, or vice versa; too thin, and there's not enough protection from emotional trespass; too thick, and you miss the cues that you're committing it yourself. (In fact, research indicates that medium permeability is a more adaptive position than either high or low.) What your scores on the Boundary Style Questionnaire provide is a snapshot of how you characteristically relate to yourself and to others—a way of seeing how the meaning you make of your inner and outer experience affects it. Just being conscious of other ways of constructing meaning can change it; for example, *having* relationships is very different from *being* them, in terms of how you feel about them as well as how you behave in them.

Without awareness and insight, the first two principles of boundary intelligence, there can be no agency. Without agency, you're limited by your boundaries; with it, you have more options for using them to get what you want and need from other people and fine-tuning the way you manage yourself in your relationships with them.

Although many people have a mixture of thick and thin boundaries, most tend to favor one or the other of these positions on the permeability continuum. Carol's outer boundaries are thicker than many women's—she keeps a certain friendly distance from everyone, enjoys working alone rather than in groups or teams, and has a companionable if not very intimate relationship with her husband. But this mathematician, whose career demands the precision that's mirrored in her personal qualities—from her well-organized home and office to her logical, analytical mind and her passion for Bach— is surprisingly available to her inner self; her thoughts, feelings, moods, and sensations tend to flow together when she's daydreaming, listening to music, or lost in a novel. It's those moments, that capability, that allow her to make theoretical leaps in her work, to put a problem aside while she reads or plays her cello, and have the answer in front of her when she goes back to her algorithms. By contrast, Hilary's outer boundaries are much more permeable than her inner ones, which account for her success as a salesperson and her ability to get along with almost anyone, but it doesn't describe her strong control of her moods and emotions, her distress when anything is out of place in her tidy, well-ordered office, or her satisfaction with a somewhat remote husband who doesn't demand much of her in the way of emotional accessibility.

What Boundary Style Means, and What It Doesn't

In creating the Boundary Style Questionnaire, I generated questions from several sources, including some sections of the Hartmann instrument, as well as other items from a number of existing psychometric instruments that tap into various aspects of boundaries, such as privacy and self-disclosure; a review of the psychological literature; and especially, long-range interviews with many people who helped me "map" the boundary concept by brainstorming, visualizing, deconstructing, and discussing it.

Social scientists evaluate self-report questionnaires and other types of instruments by how they correlate with other measures designed to assess similar constructs; how they relate to the under-lying attributes or characteristics being investigated; whether they appear to look or be valid; and by certain other criteria, such as pre-dictive value. The Boundary Style Questionnaire presented here has not yet been assessed in these ways. I devised it in order to sort, clas-sify, and make some general observations about certain kinds of emotional and interpersonal experience rather than "measure" it, so it is necessarily subjective as well as objective.

In over a hundred interviews, I tried to correlate (or not) what people said about themselves and their relationships with how they answered the questions. When there was confusion or a lack of agreement on what an item meant, I either refined it or eliminated it. When people said, "But this doesn't ask if . . . (or why, or when)," I added an item designed to get at this aspect of their experience. I started out with four hundred items and condensed or eliminated the overlapping ones. I asked people to complete some parts of the questionnaire in terms of all their relationships and then as it related to certain specific ones—with their partners, friends, family members, and colleagues. And when they completed their question-naires, I asked one last question: "Does this instrument reflect who you feel you are and what you most often experience?" When it didn't, I probed more deeply, which often led to changing the item to describe their experience more accurately.

The first step in creating a measure of a psychological construct is defining the construct to be measured. The Boundary Style Ques-tionnaire defines a theoretical universe of boundary intelligence as consisting of three dimensions: permeability, complexity, and flexi-bility. The sample of individuals consisted of a hundred-plus women between the ages of twenty-two and sixty-five, married and single, straight and lesbian, in a variety of occupations. It's what sociologists call a snowball sample—I started with women I knew, who led me to others who were willing to participate. I also sampled twenty-five men, whose questionnaires tended to support the research that indicates that overall, women's boundaries tend to be slightly (but not greatly) more permeable than men's. In order to minimize what's called "response pattern bias," where the respondent simply goes down the page without really reading the questions thoroughly and circles a "3," for instance, as a response to all the questions, I inserted some reverse-scored or negatively worded items so that a positive response indicates a "lack" of the construct, and kept the number of items to a minimum in each section.

There are five sections of the Boundary Style Questionnaire. The first three sections relate to how permeable your boundaries are in three different kinds of relationships: with yourself, with the person you're most intimately involved with, and with other people in your life. While permeability usually varies somewhat across relationships, it also has an overall tendency toward either thickness or thinness, which can be described by averaging these three scores. Looking at them individually gives you a better idea of the extent to which your boundaries in each of these areas reflect that tendency.

The fourth and fifth sections of the questionnaire relate to two other dimensions of boundaries: flexibility and complexity. These are the dimensions that connote the possibility of movement, action, and change. Flexibility describes the capacity to regulate boundary permeability and has two subdimensions, awareness and agency. While one may be aware of the need to adjust permeability, the ability to do so—agency—may be limited. Thus, agency is more closely linked to complexity, which, as we've seen, changes according to developmental stage; the more able one is to distinguish and differentiate between and among parts of the self (what is Me and what is Not Me, what is subject and what is object, what I am embedded in and what I can relate to), the more multifaceted or complex their boundaries are. Nancy Popp's research indicates that complexity and flexibility don't vary as greatly in different kinds of relationships as much as permeability does; in other words, complexity doesn't dictate boundary permeability, but it has a more significant relationship with the capacity to vary permeability.

The questions in the complexity section of the questionnaire can only roughly approximate the developmental stage; they are drawn from Kegan's and Popp's constructive developmental research that makes use of a lengthy instrument called the Subject Object interview, which bases its classification of stages on a detailed phenomenological analysis of the real-life experiences of the interviewee.

Fill out the questionnaire and total your scores in each of the sections. Then translate each of your subscores as high, medium, or low, according to the chart at the end of each section (high or low in the complexity dimension). Average the three permeability scores (inner, intimate, and interpersonal) to get a median and determine whether your overall permeability is high, medium, or low.

A cautionary note: neither the individual items nor the ranking of the scores into categories reflects the outer extremities of these dimensions; even the lowest or highest scores are within "normal" limits in terms of mental health and reflect a level of complexity, or psychological development, well past either of the stages typical of childhood and adolescence. Additionally, the positions themselves—high, medium, low—don't take into account the many gradations in and between them. But the numerical scores in each area can be useful in determining, for example, whether you're at the low end of high in one particular dimension, the high end of low in another, or mostly in the middle—what Robert Kegan calls the "evolutionary truce" (which is where you're most likely to reflect aspects of both stages of psychological growth—where you've been and where you're going).

After you've scored the questionnaire, look at the lists on the following pages to get a better idea of what your scores mean. There are eight bulleted lists, each of which describes a particular position and dimension with several descriptors typical of that particular configuration; they are the elements of your individual boundary style. Not all of these descriptors may be applicable or appropriate for you; some may not seem to resonate at all.

There are only two positions on the complexity continuum: high and low. These correspond roughly to the stages of adult development Robert Kegan calls interpersonal and institutional. Again, your actual numerical score on this section of the questionnaire is a better indication of your position on the developmental continuum than the label might suggest.

The Boundary Style Questionnaire

Inner Boundaries

Please read each answer key carefully before choosing your answer, as some of the statements are reverse-scored or negatively worded.

1. I don't know whether I'm thinking or feeling. _____
    0 = never   1 = sometimes   2 = often   3 = always

2. I like to have beautiful experiences without analyzing them. _____
    0 = never   1 = sometimes   2 = often   3 = always

3. I feel connected to a divine presence. _____
    0 = never   1 = sometimes   2 = often   3 = always

4. I lose track of what time it is. _____
    0 = never   1 = sometimes   2 = often   3 = always

5. The past is very present in my thoughts. _____
    0 = never   1 = sometimes   2 = often   3 = always

6. I feel older or younger than I am. _____
    0 = never   1 = sometimes   2 = often   3 = always

7. I fantasize and daydream. _____
    0 = never   1 = sometimes   2 = often   3 = always

8. When I read a book or see a movie, I can get so caught up in it that it can be hard to get back to reality. _____

   0 = never 1 = sometimes 2 = often 3 = always

9. My feelings are easily hurt. _____

   0 = never 1 = sometimes 2 = often 3 = always

10. If I have a problem, I reason my way through it logically and analytically. _____

    0 = always 1 = often 2 = sometimes 3 = never

Total _____

Intimate Boundaries

1. I get so involved with my intimate's problems that I lose sight of my own feelings. _____

   0 = never 1 = sometimes 2 = often 3 = always

2. I can and do tell my intimate whatever I think or feel. _____

   0 = never 1 = sometimes 2 = often 3 = always

3. How my intimate feels about me affects how I feel about myself. _____

   0 = never 1 = sometimes 2 = often 3 = always

4. Conflict with my intimate is hard on me emotionally. _____

   0 = never 1 = sometimes 2 = often 3 = always

5. When my intimate is angry or upset with me, it's hard to concentrate on anything else. _____

   0 = never 1 = sometimes 2 = often 3 = always

6. When my intimate describes a problem, I can analyze what he's saying without becoming personally involved.   _____

   0 = always   1 = often   2 = sometimes   3 = never

7. When my intimate is mad at someone, I get angry with him, too.   _____

   0 = never   1 = sometimes   2 = often   3 = always

8. After a fight with an intimate, I replay it in my head.   _____

   0 = never   1 = sometimes   2 = often   3 = always

9. I think about my intimate's problems even when they have nothing to do with me and we're not together.   _____

   0 = never   1 = sometimes   2 = often   3 = always

10. I always know who I am and who my intimate is in our relationship—I don't confuse the two.   _____

    0 = always true   1 = often true   2 = sometimes true
    3 = never true

Total   _____

Interpersonal Boundaries

1. Tact and consideration are more important between people than directness and candor.   _____

   0 = never   1 = sometimes   2 = often   3 = always

2. Conflict with others makes me anxious.   _____

   0 = never   1 = sometimes   2 = often   3 = always

3. I feel hurt when others don't understand me.   _____

   0 = never   1 = sometimes   2 = often   3 = always

4. What others think about me affects how I feel
   about myself. _____
   0 = never   1 = sometimes   2 = often   3 = always

5. I tend to keep my distance until I know I can
   trust others. _____
   0 = always   1 = often   2 = sometimes   3 = never

6. I am a very open person. _____
   0 = never   1 = sometimes   2 = often   3 = always

7. I say what I think to people even if I don't
   know them well. _____
   0 = never   1 = sometimes   2 = often   3 = always

8. My friends think they know me, but they
   really don't. _____
   0 = true   1 = often true   2 = sometimes true   3 = never true

9. I'm usually the one who compromises in a
   disagreement. _____
   0 = never   1 = sometimes   2 = often   3 = always

10. When something happens to someone I know
    or know about, it's almost as if it happened to me. _____
    0 = never   1 = sometimes   2 = often   3 = always

Total _____

To determine your boundary permeability, add your inner, intimate, and interpersonal scores. Divide this number by 3 to obtain your average score.

Total of Inner, Intimate, and Interpersonal Scores: _____

Average Score: _____

Boundary Complexity

1. I have different friends for different purposes and/or occasions.   _____

    0 = never   1 = sometimes   2 = often   3 = always

2. I leave the door open even after a relationship has ended.   _____

    0 = never   1 = sometimes   2 = often   3 = always

3. I prefer to have everything spelled out and know exactly where things stand between us in all my relationships.   _____

    0 = always   1 = often   2 = sometimes   3 = never

4. I can feel close to someone who doesn't accept all of me.   _____

    0 = never   1 = sometimes   2 = often   3 = always

5. I find it difficult to work with people I don't like or respect.   _____

    0 = always true   1 = often true   2 = sometimes true
    3 = never true

6. There are parts of my friends I can't understand or accept.   _____

    0 = always   1 = often   2 = sometimes   3 = never

7. Doing the right thing for the wrong reason, or the wrong thing for the right reason, is morally acceptable.   _____

    0 = never true   1 = sometimes true   2 = often true
    3 = always true

8. I'm responsible for my part in a relationship but not for the relationship itself.   _____

    0 = never   1 = sometimes   2 = often   3 = always

9. The more equally people share private or personal information, the better their relationship is. _____

   0 = always true   1 = often true   2 = sometimes true
   3 = never true

10. Underneath it all, people are pretty much the same. _____

    0 = always true   1 = often true   2 = sometimes true
    3 = never true

Total _____

Boundary Flexibility

1. My standards and principles don't change regardless of the person or situation. _____

   0 = always true   1 = often true   2 = sometimes true
   3 = never true

2. I'm not greatly affected by other people's moods or feelings—I can tune them out when I want or need to. _____

   0 = never   1 = sometimes   2 = often   3 = always

3. I can be very close to someone in one way and very distant or disconnected from him or her in other ways. _____

   0 = never   1 = sometimes   2 = often   3 = always

4. I choose who influences me, and how much, based on what I know about myself and what I think and feel about him or her. _____

   0 = not true   1 = sometimes true   2 = often true
   3 = always true

5. I don't tell people about myself unless they ask directly. _____

   0 = always true   1 = often true   2 = sometimes true
   3 = never true

6. I rely on feedback from others to regulate what I
   say or do.   _____
   0 = never   1 = sometimes   2 = often   3 = always

7. I don't like to reveal too much about myself, and
   I don't want to know too much about most
   other people.   _____
   0 = always true   1 = often true   2 = sometimes true
   3 = never true

8. It's hard to be around people who are in a good
   mood when I feel low or depressed.   _____
   0 = always true   1 = often true   2 = sometimes true
   3 = never true

9. With people I trust, I'm very open; with those I
   don't, I'm very careful about what I say or do.   _____
   0 = never true   1 = sometimes true   2 = often true
   3 = always true

10. There are certain lines I won't let anyone cross;
    if they do, that's it for us.   _____
    0 = always true   1 = often true   2 = sometimes true
    3 = never true

Total   _____

Scoring the Boundary Style Questionnaire

Write down your quiz scores in the spaces below.

Inner Boundaries: _____

Intimate Boundaries: _____

Interpersonal Boundaries: _____

Total Permeability Score: _____

Average Permeability Score: _____

    0–10 = Low Permeability

    11–20 = Medium Permeability

    21–30 = High Permeability

Complexity Score: _____

    0–15 = Low Complexity

    16–30 = High Complexity

Flexibility Score: _____

    0–10 = Low Flexibility

    11–20 = Medium Flexibility

    21–30 = High Flexibility

What the Scores Mean

High Permeability: More Connected Than Separate

- "There are many voices inside me, all clamoring to be heard."
- "Our two hearts beat as one."
- "My self is made up of others."

Below are qualities that describe people with high permeability.

sensitive	fragile
empathetic	intuitive
imaginative	restless
spontaneous	receptive
introspective	unguarded
gullible	idealistic

passionate	emotive
spiritual	disclosive
distractible	creative
individualistic	vulnerable
impractical	impressionable
overinvolved	inclusive
liberal	

Medium Permeability: Both Separate and Connected

- "I keep others around but not inside."

- "I will not lose myself in you or us."

- "I can see myself through others' eyes without losing sight of myself."

The following are characteristics of people with medium permeability.

adaptable	candid/tactful
responsive	reciprocal
reflective	approachable
friendly	consistent
temperate	prudent
mutual	engaging
circumspect	logical
self-monitoring	synthesizer
balanced	self-protecting
traditional	

Low Permeability: More Separate Than Connected

- "I keep others away."

- "I am who I am."

- "This close and no closer."

Low-permeability people often exhibit these qualities.

constrained	resolute
impenetrable	explicit
focused	orderly
self-contained	concrete
nonexpressive	exclusive
persistent	judgmental
self-reliant	decisive
self-constructed	disciplined
disengaged	underwhelmed
masked	consistent

Low (Interpersonal) Complexity

- "I am my relationships."
- "Your experience of me tells me who I am."
- "How open I am depends on you."
- "If we don't feel the same way, I don't feel whole."
- "I don't know where your feelings end and mine begin."
- "I can't prioritize conflicting expectations or loyalties."
- "It's hard to hold onto my position if yours is different."
- "Your presence or absence is necessary to hold me together."
- "I need your feedback to know myself."
- "I can't keep my feelings inside."
- "When you criticize my behavior, I feel like a bad person."
- "Either you know all of me, or you don't know me at all."
- "I handle internal conflict by displacing it on part of it in you."

- "I can't want someone who rejects me."
- "I'm responsible for our relationship."
- "You decide where the limits are drawn and maintained."
- "I rely on cues from you to regulate my permeability."
- "Your needs and expectations control my sense of appropriateness."

High (Institutional) Complexity

- "I generate my own values and expectations."
- "My identity comes from inside of me."
- "It's okay if you only know part of me."
- "I take cues from you, but I manage my response myself."
- "We can have different needs and agendas and still connect."
- "I define myself by what I know of myself and my inner process."
- "I'm not responsible for your feelings."
- "I have my relationships."
- "Our interaction or process is the means to an end."
- "I'm responsible for my part in our relationship."
- "I decide where the limits are drawn and maintained."
- "I rely on my feelings to regulate my permeability."
- "I consider my needs and yours independently to decide what's appropriate."
- "I can separate and relate to my competing feelings and loyalties."
- "I can relate to some parts of you but not others."

- "I'm not invested in my way of running things."

- "I don't need to defend my self-system against yours."

- "The process or interaction isn't the means, it's the end itself."

Flexibility

pliant	adaptable
malleable	supple
changeable	contextual
fluid	energetic
alterable	responsive
dynamic	adjustable
dialectical	variable
inconstant	

HIGH FLEXIBILITY

A person with high flexibility

- Is easily able to regulate permeability

- Has the greatest range between openness and closedness

- Relies on cues from self, environment, context to open up or close down, let out self, and/or let others in

- Adjusts permeability depending on sense of safety or threat to self

MEDIUM FLEXIBILITY

People with medium flexibility

- Have a moderate ability to regulate permeability

- Are committed to a certain range of openness between self and others

- Rely on feedback from others based on rules, roles, and context to open up or close down, let out self, and/or let others in

- Adjust permeability depending on rules that govern a situation or relationship

LOW FLEXIBILITY

Someone with low flexibility

- Has a minimal capacity to regulate permeability

- Is stuck in an open or closed position

- Can alter permeability slightly but feels unsafe doing so

Two Boundary Styles

On the following pages are two boundary maps for Libby and Janet. As you can see from their scores, Libby and Janet have very different boundary styles. Janet's boundaries are much more permeable than Libby's, but they're not as flexible or as complex, even though on that dimension, there's only a difference of two points on their scores.

The variance in their boundary styles is readily apparent to those who know both women. Libby is a highly organized and efficient person who isn't particularly self-reflective: "I'm not one of those people who's into navel gazing," she says, "and I don't have much tolerance for those who are." She's more permeable to other people, especially her husband; she comes across as open and friendly, although she can adjust her boundaries more successfully and on a more piecemeal basis than Janet, whose significantly more limited flexibility hinders her capacity to regulate her permeability. Both women take their cues from others about when to be more or less open or closed, although Libby's higher scores on the complexity continuum indicate that if she were more aware of her internal

Libby's Boundary Map

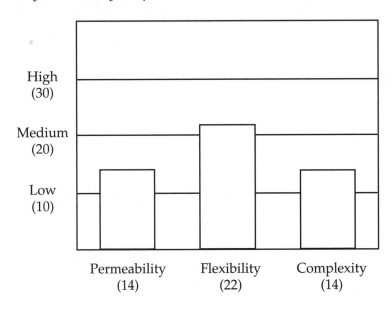

Permeability (14)   Flexibility (22)   Complexity (14)

Permeability Breakdown

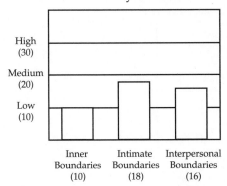

Inner Boundaries (10)   Intimate Boundaries (18)   Interpersonal Boundaries (16)

Libby's Boundary Style

Medium Permeability: Both separate and connected: "I keep others around but not inside."

High Flexibility: Easily able to regulate permeability.

Low Complexity: "I rely on cues from you to regulate my permeability."

Janet's Boundary Map

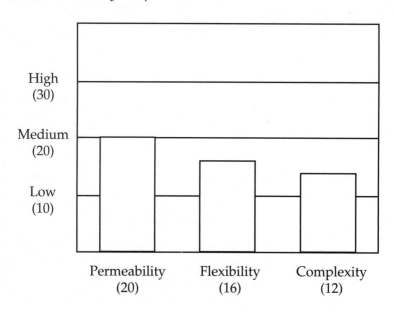

Permeability (20)   Flexibility (16)   Complexity (12)

Permeability Breakdown

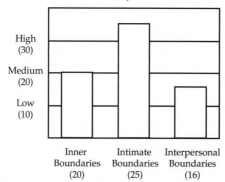

Inner Boundaries (20)   Intimate Boundaries (25)   Interpersonal Boundaries (16)

Janet's Boundary Style

High Permeability: More connected than separate: "My self is made up of others."

Medium Flexibility: Moderate ability to regulate permeability.

Low Complexity: "I am my relationships."

process (especially her feelings), she'd be able to make those choices based on what she wants and needs as well as what the other person demands or desires and what general rather than context-specific "rules of engagement" apply.

In terms of developmental stage, as Libby's numbers indicate, she's capable of differentiating her own voice from the voices within her and relating to other people on some levels even if she doesn't like or isn't interested in other aspects of their personality. She's usually able to maintain her position when faced with opposition, especially from her colleagues, but when the conflict is with her husband or her mother or even her teenage son, she's more likely to back down. It seems from her scores that developmentally she's closer to the institutional complexity stage than to the interpersonal one—the numbers reflect the "evolutionary truce" between those two positions, and when she circles the statements in the complexity lists that do and do not apply to her, she can see where she needs to shift her consciousness to improve her ability to tolerate competing expectations and loyalties and listen for internal cues as well as input from others to regulate her permeability.

Janet, whose permeability is significantly higher overall than Libby's, is relaxed and uninhibited with almost everyone. She says whatever comes into her head without thinking much about it, and she loves not wisely but too well, which accounts for the multitude of intimate relationships she's had. She has much more difficulty than Libby does in tuning out the psychological influence of other people: "Sometimes it seems like my transmitter is always set on 'receive,'" she says, which means that any kind of negative feedback cuts her to the quick. She comes across as open and unguarded, even in situations where it might be wiser to keep her own counsel and protect her vulnerability. She's much more aware of internal conflict than Libby is, but she's less able to regulate it without projecting or assigning it to others. She can distinguish the members of her "committee" from her own sense of herself, but she has a harder time managing and integrating them than Libby does and often has difficulty knowing herself without feedback from others. She, too, is in an evolutionary truce between two different ways of organizing her experience: "I'd like to have more control over my relationships rather than be at their mercy," she says. But just being aware of the difference allows her to manage herself more effectively in them.

In the following chapters, we'll look at where inner, intimate, and interpersonal boundaries come from, and how yours affect your relationships with your parents and siblings; your partner, spouse, and children as well as your in-laws and ex-laws; your good, better, and best friends; and your professional colleagues. While psychoanalytic and object relations theory provide the underpinnings of these explanations, you don't have to be a psychologist to understand them or appreciate that while important relationships in the past provide an emotional template for your present ones, growth is a lifelong process and boundary style is an evolutionary one. In other words, history isn't necessarily destiny, but the more aware you are of your own history, the more capable you are of changing the way you relate to the past in order to deal more effectively with the present.

CHAPTER 4

Where Do Our Boundaries
Come From?

Where do our boundaries—and our boundary style—come from? Are we born with them fully formed, or do our earliest experiences give them shape and meaning? We land, as John Updike has written, "on the shores of our own beginning in total innocence, and it takes decades to penetrate inland and map the mountain passes and trace the rivers to their sources." And while it's not necessary to make that arduous journey in order to understand what's going on in your life right now, a glance backward can't hurt.

If this isn't the first self-help book you've picked up—if you've ever taken a psych course, been in therapy, browsed the personal growth or New Age section at a bookstore, or discovered a paradigm, label, or explanation that seems to fit you—you may already have a "story" or psychological narrative about who you are and how you got that way.

Deirdre, a thirty-seven-year-old whose intimate relationships include one marriage, two living-together arrangements, a couple of summer loves, and several passionate but brief affairs, attributes her mistrust of men to her father's desertion. "It's like I have this script titled *All Men Leave*, and if they don't follow it, I get so anxious waiting for the sword to fall that I'm the one who cuts and runs," she says. She's presently keeping company with a guy who's exceptionally understanding about her fear of commitment: "I have unpacked my emotional baggage with him, which he understands because his dad deserted him, too; he's come a lot further in making peace with his past than I have, so he's very patient with me. He's almost convinced me that he's going to hang in for the long haul. I'm not quite there yet, but I'm determined not to screw this one up, and we're talking about going to couples counseling together just to make sure of it."

Heidi identifies herself as the adult child of alcoholics: "I grew up never knowing whether I was going to be kissed or kicked," she says. "Not literally—I wasn't physically abused. But I had to sort of tiptoe around my parents until I knew what to expect—what kind of mood they were in, whether they were going to be fighting, if they'd remembered they were supposed to take me somewhere or come to a conference at school, whether I could have a friend over without worrying how they'd behave. The one incident that stands out among all the others is my fourteenth birthday. I'd invited eight friends to a sleepover party, and about an hour before they were supposed to arrive, my parents mixed a pitcher of cocktails, and within fifteen minutes they were screaming at each other and ripping up the party decorations. When I asked them to stop, they got furious with me; my mother picked up my birthday cake and threw it on the floor!" Heidi ran upstairs and called her best friend. "I told her my grandmother had just died, so I had to cancel the party; she said she'd call everyone else and tell them." When Heidi's mother had a stroke years later—on Heidi's daughter's tenth birthday—she went ahead with the party anyway. "I didn't even tell my husband until after everyone left; all the while I was singing 'Happy Birthday' to Amelia I was thinking, I'm not going to let my mother ruin one more happy occasion for me!"

Dash says her need to please derives from being a middle child. "My sister was the temperamental one—she was always fighting with my folks. My brother was the baby, and the only boy, so he got all the attention lavished on him. I just never felt like anyone cared about me, no matter how good I was. And boy, was I good—I never did one rebellious thing, I got straight A's in school, and when my mother got cancer, I was the one who left college and came home to take care of her . . . there was just never any question that I would." In her own family, she continued to try to satisfy everyone else's needs instead of her own. "It might not have been so bad if people noticed it or even, God forbid, thanked me! But they just took it for granted, so I felt not only exhausted, both physically and emotionally, but totally overlooked and unseen."

One day Dash saw a flyer about an assertiveness training course at the community college where she teaches. "I believe that if you're ready to ask the questions, the answers are there for you to find. But it has to be the right question at least some of the time—'What can I do to make myself happier?' not 'What can I do to make everyone else happier?' Something about the way the flyer was worded just rang a bell in me. I got a lot of resistance from my family when I started speaking up for myself, but now they're used to it, and they don't just take it for granted that they can dump their bad moods on me, or expect me to jolly them out of them, or, in the case of my grown kids, continue to sacrifice myself to make them happy, or pour on the tea and sympathy when they're not, especially when what they really need is a kick in the butt!"

It's human nature to displace the responsibility for our shortcomings, insecurities, or lack of control wherever we can, and almost everyone's childhood offers plenty of reasons to explain and even justify their adult behavior. As long as Bette blames her excess poundage on her mother's habit of using food as a reward for good behavior when Bette was a child, she never has to deny herself a chocolate éclair. Since Karla's father was a miser who not only "saved every nickel until it squeaked" but demanded that she turn over to him whatever she earned by babysitting or dog walking, she feels justified in spending every dime of her six-figure salary, and more, even if the result is bankruptcy; after all, it's not her fault. On the other hand, Grete blames her explosive temper and inability to sustain an intimate relationship on being a red-headed Scorpio—that's her story, and she's sticking to it!

Even when the actual experiences of the past have faded, their emotional imprint remains and provides the "arc" of our psychological narrative. It colors how we interpret what happened to us—whatever we can consciously, if hazily, recall learning, seeing, hearing, or feeling that we believe influenced who we are today, like Judith's mother's depression or Emma's father's abuse or even Susannah's adoption (although it happened when she was less than a week old). Emotional memory carries the "charge" of events or experiences forward in time, so even if what occurred is forgotten, the emotions that remain are exactly the same as what they were then, especially if we were scared, hurt, ignored, confused, or humiliated. And when something happens today that stimulates those same feelings, emotional memory—the part of us that psychoanalysts call the subconscious or the observing ego, neuroscientists call the limbic brain, and I call Small Mind—makes a connection between then and now, even if on the surface there doesn't seem to be one. Like Deirdre's anxiety about intimacy and commitment, Heidi's need for the control she never had as a child, and Dash's self-esteem, which depended on pleasing others, emotional memory colors how we respond to current events, even when they don't seem to bear much resemblance to those in our childhood past.

Any shrink worth his Eames chair can cite chapter and verse about experiences and conditions that tend to affect psychological development. You don't have to be a rocket scientist to realize that certain childhood scenarios, especially extreme ones such as abandonment or abuse, are likely to result in emotional problems later in life, even for highly resilient individuals who seem to be born with certain innate characteristics that protect them from the worst effects of trauma and stress, like Maya.

Maya was six when her parents fled a refugee camp in Vietnam and made their way to America after a long, terror-filled journey.

She had already learned a little English in the camp and became the interface between her parents and their bewildering new world. Despite experiences that might have made another child wary of strangers, she was a buoyant, cheerful girl with a knack for making friends. Her adolescence was marked by traumas that would have daunted a less resilient person—her mother's remarriage to a violent man, her rape by her stepfather, her younger brother's murder in a drive-by shooting, and finally a fire that destroyed the few belongings the family had managed to accumulate. Yet Maya doesn't dwell on the past—she rarely even refers to it and explains her remarkable achievements by saying, "We Hmong, we're like weeds . . . give us a cup of dirt and a little bit of sunshine, we push up even through cement. When your parents risk their lives to give you the chance for a better future, you don't worry about what they didn't give you," she says. "If someone holds out their hand to you, you take it; you don't say, 'Oh, please, I need both your hands, one isn't enough.' You pull yourself up and then you reach out with your free hand and pull up somebody else."

Maya counts herself lucky: "No matter how bad off you are, there's always someone who's worse," she says. "If I have a 'story,' if my past has meaning, that's what it is."

Most psychodynamic theories explain behavior in adult relationships by a retroactive analysis of personal history; cause and effect, after all, is the sine qua non of science. But as Dr. Robert Kegan observes, psychological development is more than just a regressive replay of early events. Like boundaries, it's an ongoing, evolutionary process rather than a fixed, permanent product of the past. Although the phenomena of infancy and childhood may be represented in your boundary style, they're not its only determinant, or even the most relevant one. By adulthood you have a life history of self-other relationships whose accumulated meaning influences your current ones as much if not more than your earliest ones.

It's still worthwhile, however, to revisit your own history, review what you can surmise or infer about where your basic boundary style came from, and understand that boundaries are made and remade in every relationship, not just according to what happens in the present but what happened in the past—or at least, what *feels* like what happened.

I Relate, Therefore I Am

Does relationship—the experience of others—call the self into being, or does the self already exist? The answer depends on which psychological church you worship at. While Freud viewed the self as a collection of drives and instincts, developed through the internal processes of maturation, psychosocial and object-relations theorists who came after him believed that the self is organized and held together by relationship; development is shaped by interaction with other people, especially, in the beginning, the mother (or, in these enlightened times, the primary caretaker). In fact, as Donald Winnicott, one of the most prominent object-relations psychologists (who was also a pediatrician) observed, "There is no such thing as [just] an infant."

Without begging the old question of which came first, the chicken or the egg, it seems likely that as soon as an infant consciousness exists that can construct a rough mental approximation of two entities—Me and Not Me—there is a conceptual boundary between them. Psychologists differ on how early in life this occurs, but most agree that the constancy or stability of that initial boundary is a process, not a single event. The boundary creates the distinction between self and other; it is as essential to wholeness and relatedness as is figure to ground, form to content, structure to resonance. Individual difference—the constitutional endowment that makes us by nature stolid or sensitive, nervous or calm, thin-skinned or unflappable, placid or curious—has as much to do with boundary style as it does with personality; physiology may not be entirely destiny, but spend a few minutes in a hospital nursery and you'll notice that some babies seem to experience their environment, including other people, as comfortable and tolerable, while others appear to be stressed or overwhelmed by it.

Regardless of how sensitive or responsive we are to the emotional "surround" and social environment of early life, the themes of infancy and childhood echo through all of our subsequent relationships—themes like safety, trust, recognition, and stability (if we were lucky), and insecurity, instability, invisibility, or isolation (if we weren't). Unconsciously, or even with some measure of insight or awareness, depending on how alive the past is in our present or how permeable the boundary between them is, our most significant adult relationships bear the psychological imprint of our earliest ones. They may not replicate our first ones precisely—they may even reflect the conscious desire not to resemble them at all—but they always retain some aspect of them. And so do the boundaries that define them.

The Narcissistic Fix

Boundary style, like other aspects of development, depends on nurture as well as nature. As our bodies cohere and begin to register sensations within the limiting membrane of our skin, we look into our mother's face, see ourselves reflected in her eyes, and begin to know *that*, if not yet *who*, we are. We make the meaning of our being from her being—her smell, touch, gaze, smile, frown, and feel. Slowly we evolve from being *the same as* to being *at one with*. It's the rupture of the amniotic boundary that makes us human, but it's its psychic counterpart, begun in the first weeks of life and continued thereafter, that makes us human beings. We are made "real" to our infant selves by adequate mirroring from parents who reflect our physical and emotional essence back to us: *Oh, this is who I am, this being who makes her coo and smile and notice that I'm hungry/wet/need to be held.* But it will be months before *one* becomes *two*, before that first boundary—*separate from*—is truly real to both mother and child. An old Hasidic expression reflects that reality: If I am I because you are you, and if you are you because I am I, then I am not I and you are not you.

This first actual *experience* of a boundary, and its affect—how it *feels* to be separate—colors our experience with subsequent boundaries. Insufficiently mirrored for whatever reason, we may spend our lives seeking someone to affirm that we exist, or numb ourselves to our own needs and deny them ever after. Lacy's mother sunk into a depression shortly after she was born, which left her incapable of providing the narcissistic fix necessary for her child to develop a confident, inner self-love. Lacy has spent the last two decades attempting to be "seen" by others, especially men: "There is the false self—really, a whole series of them—that I put on when I meet someone, and if he doesn't like that one, I try a different one out on him. I guess I think that if I ever show the real me to a guy— if I even know who the real me is anymore—he'll just bolt." Lacy doesn't remember the first time her mother held her or even if she did. Mostly what she recalls are the words she heard over and over again as a child, even if she can't grab onto the reasons for them: "They must have given me the wrong baby at the hospital because I can't imagine where you came from—you're nothing like me! Why can't you do anything right?" She adds, "I think at some time every kid has the fantasy that her parents aren't really her parents, but most parents don't play into it like my mother did. I never felt like I belonged in my family . . . or anywhere else, for that matter."

It's this love of self that makes it possible, later, to love others. But if we don't get enough mirroring from our first others, we can't ever do that; although we keep looking for something that's missing, we can't always identify what it is, since in future relationships it may pose as admiration, power, love, or authenticity—whatever makes us feel whole, perfect, filled up, safe, real, special.

It Won't Bother Me If You Leave

While existence depends on attachment, growth requires the ability to separate. What makes this possible is a mental representation of the mother or the caretaker, developed by the baby in his or her first year and a half of life—a sort of internalized working model that produces the same sense of comfort and security as the mother's actual presence. A securely attached child can allow his or her mother to separate, confident that she will return. But if that internalized presence isn't either consistent or comforting, the child's emotional template for subsequent separations, not only from his or her mother but also from other significant people, may feel like abandonment.

It's not what happens to us but the meaning we make of it that structures our story—our psychological narrative—and provides our raison d'être, the (seemingly) logical explanation for why we feel, believe, and behave as we do. Although the lines of emotional development stretch all the way back to the earliest experiences with the first other in our life, the meaning we attach to relationship derives from how we experienced ourselves not only with that person but also with the rest of those who peopled our first social world and the impressions they left on us.

All in the Family

The family is the container for development where we play out the drama of attachment and separation over and over, a drama expressed as fusion and differentiation that reflects our needs for connection and belonging as well as individuation and autonomy. Every family boundary style reflects a place on that continuum.

If boundaries within your family were weak or enmeshed, as they were in Randi's, you probably didn't feel entitled to have your own ideas or feelings: "I grew up needing others to tell me what to think or how to feel, which is probably why I let people do it now," she says. "I tend to take it for granted that they know me better than I know myself, even when there's this little voice inside me whispering, 'But that's not true!'"

In Rose's enmeshed family, her mother spoke for everyone—including Rose's father. Overly involved with Rose's and her siblings' activities and problems, her mother's relationship with her husband took a distant second place. "My mother didn't tolerate or encourage differences of opinion or respect anyone's personal secrets and privacy," Rose remembers. "It was always us against the world, which really meant Mama against the world—we were just an extension of her. She used to tell us, family is the only thing you can trust, and when my father left her for another woman, she refused to let him see us; she said we might have his last name, but he wasn't our family any longer."

Marilou's family's internal boundaries were just as enmeshed as Rose's, and their external boundaries were just as rigidly maintained, the better to protect the family's secrets—alcoholism and sexual abuse. "I never told anyone, because I knew that would mean I'd lose them—not just my parents, but my younger sisters, too. It wasn't until my father and brother started abusing them that I actually talked to a school counselor about it. And what I'd feared would happen, did—the girls still treat me like I betrayed them, and my mother's even worse."

Parva's immigrant family "lived in each other's pockets—inside the house, there were no boundaries, no secrets, no separation." But outside there were plenty, expressed in the distance her parents kept from the world in order to shut out the influence of their adopted culture, traditions, and distractions. The first member of her family to go to college, Parva was all but ostracized by her parents and kin, who viewed her social and intellectual growth as a betrayal of their values and an indication of disloyalty to her roots. "Even though I understood it intellectually, I couldn't accept it emotionally," she says of the disengagement from her family. "I couldn't share my academic successes with them, which meant I couldn't be proud of them myself. I couldn't get close to anyone outside our small community, and I grew up ashamed of my origins. I felt just what they said I was—disloyal. It was like an actual loss of my self."

Enmeshed or fused family boundaries influence your adult boundary style. You may find it hard to balance thinking and feeling or separate reason from emotion or impulse from action or even fantasy from reality, which are expressed in highly permeable inner boundaries. In intimate relationships, you may look to a partner to fulfill your needs for recognition and self-esteem and take on his feelings instead of experiencing your own. In interpersonal ones, you may be extremely susceptible to your emotional "surround" and find it difficult to resist the psychological "force field" of others unless you're flexible enough to limit your permeability to them. At the other extreme, if your family boundaries were rigid or impermeable, you probably felt isolated, unsupported, and unappreciated when you were a kid, and still may feel that way.

"I guess I just withdrew from the world of emotions, because no one seemed to be interested in mine," says Page. "They just weren't something we talked about. My father was an engineer and my mother a scientist—their world was very orderly, rational, mechanistic, and thinking-based rather than feeling-based. Like, when my father lost his job he just pretended to go to work every day until he found another one, but we didn't know that until much later. When my sister got pregnant at sixteen, they were much more concerned with what people would think than how she might feel; in fact, after they threw her out of the house, her name was never mentioned. And when my brother was killed in the first Gulf war, they just retreated into themselves—not together, but separately. My father told me not to cry at the funeral, because that would be unpatriotic—like it would give comfort to the enemy! I wasn't even allowed to stay home from school—I went from the cemetery to my classes."

Early on, Page learned the habit of denying her emotions the way her parents did. By the time she married Ben, she had little real sense of her own feelings and was blissfully unaware of his. When their marriage ended, he told her he couldn't continue to live with her "insensitivity" any longer. Up to that point, she says, "I had no inkling that my marriage was in trouble; it felt like I'd had the rug pulled out from under me." Emotions are still largely terra incognita to Page, which is reflected in her boundary style, which is low in both permeability and flexibility. She believes the challenge of getting her denied and repressed feelings "out of the closet and into the light" is beyond her. "Maybe my mother was right," she adds. "She used to say, 'Feelings are so messy!'"

Eleanor also grew up in a family with rigid boundaries: "My mother's mantra was, 'We're just very private people,' which was a kind of snobby attitude when you think about it—and yes, she was a snob. Appearances were extremely important to her; to put it crudely, it was as if her shit didn't smell! We never dealt directly with things—we certainly didn't share our feelings or interact in any real way with people outside the family . . . or even with each other."

When Eleanor met Jeb, she was overwhelmed by his family—not surprising, considering her own. "Everyone knew everyone else's business and felt no compunction about commenting on it. There was no such thing as a private thought or a secret—you might hold back, but you couldn't hold out long against them . . . there were simply no boundaries at all! I think Jeb was attracted to me simply because I was so different from them; he used to say that he loved what he called my 'reserve.' But almost as soon as we were married, he kept pushing me to tell him what I was feeling or thinking, and then tell me why I shouldn't feel or think that way . . . and mostly what I started feeling was suffocated! Even though he and I both thought he was different from them, he wasn't." In order to make their marriage work, they both had to find a way to live with the boundary styles shaped by their childhood experiences; Eleanor needed to adjust her permeability to allow Jeb access to her inner world, and Jeb to accept that some aspects of it are unavailable to him, or even to Eleanor herself. Keeping his more forceful and voluble emotions from overwhelming Eleanor, he's learning to respect her right to have her own. "We're still trying to find a middle ground that works for us," she says. "Intimacy still isn't easy for me, but I'm getting better at it."

In Judith Guest's resonant novel *Ordinary People*, the Jarrett family boundaries have become so rigid and brittle since the death of Buck, the adored and idealized eldest son, that no connection is possible among the survivors. Conrad, the troubled teenager, feels he has no right to exist; he retreats inside, even attempts suicide, to defend himself against his mother Beth's impermeable exterior, which masks the chaos within her. And Cal, the failed husband and father of the story, is emotionally adrift because he cannot understand or protect the people he loves. The Jarretts' conflicting and confused family boundaries are most clearly evident in Cal's response to Beth's fury after he tells a friend that Conrad has been in a mental hospital: "Whose privacy did I violate? His? Yours? Ours?"

How We Coped, Then and Now

As adults our boundary style reflects to some extent not only how fused or differentiated our family's boundaries were but also what we needed to do to survive emotionally inside that system. Helen's parents had a difficult and tumultuous relationship; her role was to relieve the stress in it by ministering to their emotional needs—her mother's for sympathy, her father's for affection. Vanessa's father couldn't manage his anger at the circumstances of his life, so he took it out on her; Roberta couldn't handle her jealousy of her more attractive, popular peers, so she displaced it onto her prettier sister, Polly, who never went through an awkward stage or lacked a close circle of friends. Megan had to meet her mother's narcissistic needs for validation and approval by being perfect in every respect. And if

Belle hadn't submitted to her father's sexual advances, she knew she couldn't protect her younger sisters from them.

At least, that's the theory and usually the practice, too. But in life, as in psychology, the opposite scenario may unfold later on as we attempt, consciously or unconsciously, to get in other relationships what we got too much or too little of in our earliest ones.

Big Mind, Small Mind, and Family Rules

Boundaries are shaped not only by interactions with parents and siblings but by family rules, explicitly or implicitly transmitted, that influence our ideas and behavior, determine how power is distributed, what kind of communication is encouraged, and who speaks or thinks or feels for the family. These rules reinforce messages we absorbed before we understood them; messages like those in Rose's family—don't speak the truth, don't express real feelings—or in Parva's—don't betray your traditions, get too big for your britches, forget your place, or grow beyond your beginnings.

Family rules usually reflect the values, beliefs, roles, obligations, identifications, and expectations constituted by gender, culture, generation, education, class, religion, and ethnicity—the social environment we were raised in that I call Big Mind. Even if by now we've modified or rejected some or all of Big Mind's influence, it still affects our adult judgments about other people; the appropriate, safe, or comfortable distance between us and them; and even whether and what kind of relationship we might have with someone whose values or background are different from ours.

How each of us views the world depends on the power and focus of the individual lens and the way that lens was first ground, as the writer Judith Guest says; that's also true of how we experience relationships outside the family and what aspects of them we internalize and make part of the self and those we reject—the views and opinions of teachers, peers, and friends about our importance, intelligence, attractiveness, or trustworthiness.

Both our social relationships with actual others and our inner relationships with internalized others (or parts of them) determine how boundaries feel to us—as important and necessary, protecting our independence and autonomy, or as isolating, alien, and threatening to our equilibrium. Our boundary style reflects whether we orient our emotional compass outside in enmeshed relationships with actual others or inside, according to our own needs and feelings. Directly or indirectly, we seek in relationships—especially our most intimate ones—what was psychologically or actually absent or too overwhelming to cope with when we were very young. But once we experience ourselves with other people, in other environments, who and what feels like part of us and who and what doesn't changes. This reorganization of self happens over and over, at different times in our emotional development and in different relationships throughout our lives. And every time it occurs, our boundaries change, too, which puts us in the temporary limbo of not knowing who we are or who we might become.

One of the Gang

The expanding social world of childhood offers new identifications besides those acquired in the family. Each new alliance, membership, and relationship reorganizes our sense of self and adjusts our boundaries accordingly. One of the best literary allusions to this is Stephen Dedalus's in *A Portrait of the Artist As a Young Man*, who as a child in primary school identifies himself on the flyleaf of his geography book according to the systems of which he as an individual is a part:

> Stephen Dedalus
>
> Class of Elements

Clongowes Wood College

Sallins

County Kildare

Ireland

Europe

The World

The Universe

Some of the identifications that result from our early relationships become stable, permanent parts of the self, and some are tran-
sitory. We will not always be the teacher's pet (or nemesis), a
member of the softball team, or Tiffany's best friend, even if we
retain as part of our self-concept some meaningful aspect of those
relationships, like the feeling of being considered special (in either a
good or a bad way), of belonging, cooperating, and competing
(unless we were always the last kid chosen), or being desirable
(until Tiffany dumped us for a new best friend). As we get older, we
place ourselves in the context of a group—a grade-school class, a
Brownie troop, a team, or a club—at an emotional and physical distance from our families. In each one, another set of identifications
awaits us. In middle childhood, we assimilate many of Big Mind's
identifications and the boundaries related to them, which come in
forms like rules, norms, roles, and expectations, remnants of which
endure even if as adults we've rejected them. As Rebecca says, "You
can take the girl out of parochial school, but you can't take Our Lady
of Perpetual Succor out of her, especially when you're having
unsanctified sex." Tasha, who's a big corporate honcho now but
grew up in the ghetto, knows she doesn't have to be just seen but not
heard any longer, and she doesn't have to be deferential toward her
white colleagues simply because of the color of their skin. But she
still has to steel herself to put her opinions forward, especially in
groups where she's the only person of color.

Until the end of early childhood—around six—we don't have

the mental organization to comprehend that other people have their own independent purposes; from our perspective, which is the only one we can take, others exist primarily to fulfill our needs. In middle childhood, we recognize that others may have a different point of view, and although we can make deals or plans with them and manipulate them on behalf of our own goals (*I'll be really, really good if you let me stay up late*), we can't yet hold on to both perspectives simultaneously. Until we've developed the mental capacity to be aware of shared feelings, agreements, and expectations, we can't really sustain interpersonal relationships.

Rescued from Limbo

In adolescence, we find ourselves in limbo again, not certain of who we are or will be. Like Augie March, the hero of Saul Bellow's eponymous novel, we touch all sides, and nobody knows where we belong; we may have no good idea of that ourselves. By then we've reached the stage where we can share with others at an internal as well as external level. The result is the development of a capacity for empathy and mutuality. It is this greater emotional depth, this intersubjectivity, that makes adolescent relationships so intense: "Sometimes I don't know if I'm feeling my own feelings or Susan's," says thirteen-year-old Audrey about her best friend. "It's like they're catching. When she's sad, so am I. And when she's happy, I'm happy, too." Relationships become more complex when we share emotions as well as experiences. But as we soon learn, empathy is not the same as mutuality, and mutuality is not the same as total union, which is why Audrey felt so betrayed when Susan went to Jenny's birthday party, to which Audrey hadn't been invited.

Disembedding ourselves from our families, separating from our parents, we need new others to attach to. The heroes we idealize as teenagers represent perfection and omnipotence, qualities we once believed our parents embodied and wanted to possess or control ourselves. Those we admire and identify with in adolescence have other attributes, knowledge, or skills we want to emulate or imitate. Although both idealization and identification contain some aspects of relatedness, they don't necessarily require an actual presence—these are one-sided relationships in which we take or absorb what we need to solidify our own identity. As adults, we may look back and see how certain identifications influenced the directions our lives took, our values and behavior, even how we became more (or less) like one parent than we expected to, but successful identifications are often so well integrated into our personalities that they seem like they've always been part of us.

Off with the Old, On with the New

The first way teenagers define who they are is by rejecting who they're not, staking out a place in a new system populated not by families but by peers. Investing perfection and omnipotence in our heroes, borrowing the qualities we admire from our role models, we still need real people to attach to, friends whose loyalty, reliability, and affection we can count on. Asserting our right to a separate existence is thrilling, but it is also terrifying. We are overwhelmed by the need to find ourselves in another, to feel "like" someone else, to fit in somewhere. Being a teenager, says fifteen-year-old Martina, "is like always working a jigsaw puzzle, holding yourself up against other people, turning yourself inside out and around and around, looking for the place where you belong. Lots of times there are pieces of you that don't fit anywhere." The need to fit in may require the temporary or even permanent suppression of some of those pieces. "Who doesn't remember how lonely and uncool it was to be the smartest kid in the freshman class, even though it was fine in eighth grade?" says Andrea, who rues the fact that once she got to high school she renounced not only her straight-A average but also her strong competitive streak: "Boys didn't like girls who hit home runs," she says. "I had to learn to bunt."

Disengaging from the boundaries of family, we become part of a greater whole, a tribe of peers connected by ties of friendship rather than blood, more fused than differentiated (at least in the aggregate), defined by our likenesses rather than our dissimilarities. Within that tribe we find our soul mates, with whom we share our hopes, fears, and passions, tell our darkest secrets, and pledge undying loyalty. We use our friends to discover, confirm, and consolidate who we are, putting boundaries around these first truly intersubjective relationships with rituals, secrets, and promises that reflect our expectation that they will maintain the "we" of our relationship by tending the pieces of us they carry around now—our shared feelings—just as we tend and carry theirs. But adolescent friendships are rife with disappointments, betrayals, and rejections, narcissistic injuries that lodge in Small Mind, which imprints the emotional residue of those hurts on our future relationships. Will we ever again be able to trust another person to safeguard our confidences, respect our limits, accept our limitations, and not be overwhelmed by our feelings of envy and competition as well as need and love? More important, will we ever be able to trust our own judgment about another person's reliability, or even our intuition, that part of knowing and experiencing that resides outside awareness?

By the time we've navigated the rocky shoals of adolescence, we've been in many different relationships, accumulating enough experiences of distance and closeness to know where on that continuum we feel most or least comfortable, in what circumstances, and with whom. We've left home and lived with friends and roommates. We know what it is to need our own space, physically, socially, and emotionally, or to have too much of it. We've fallen in and out of love and experienced sexual intimacy—sometimes even with the same person! In our same-sex friendships, we've suppressed, enacted, or come to terms with our normal but mostly unconscious bisexual tendencies; in our cross-sex ones, we've made our peace (or not) with heterosexual lust, as the writer Judith Viorst puts it. We've learned that love and envy, love and competition, can coexist in a friendship, although not always easily. We've felt the ambivalence between the need for connection and the desire for autonomy in ourselves, even if we can't always recognize it in other people, especially when they want more or less of one or the other than we do. We have let go of the expectation that in all but the perfect relationship we will find exactly the right balance of distance and closeness, because until we're in it, we won't really know where that is. And even then—especially then—the themes of our first and most intimate ones will be playing again.

If development stopped in early adulthood, so would the structure and style of our boundaries. But they change both physically and psychologically over our life span, just as we do. In the context of our roles as partners, spouses, parents, colleagues, friends, and adult children, we continue to discriminate between what feels like Me and what doesn't. In all these and other roles, we enlarge our capacity for relating to ourselves as well as to others—if our boundary style allows it. But if our boundaries can't adapt to the expected as well as unpredictable changes that will happen whether we welcome them or not, it may be more stressful than we expect.

CHAPTER 5

Family Whether We Like It or Not

There are no perfect parents, even fewer who never fail their kids in some way. Their sins of omission or commission and even their shortcomings have little to do with how much they loved you or how hard they tried to do their best by you. You can pay a shrink to listen or bore a friend with details of their failings forever, but why bother? The past is in the past, and you can't change it: you can only change how you relate to it. You will never have the perfect childhood you still wish you had, with parents who were always (or even often) perfectly attuned to your needs and nature. You may never have (or be) the parents you dream of even now—the ones who never take liberties, never invade their children's boundaries, never take advantage of (or revert to) the unbalanced relationship that prevails when one is small, powerless, and dependent and the other is big, powerful, and responsible.

The truth is that emotional trespass is a fact of family life, and as such, a difficult habit to break. If you doubt that, try this exercise: for one twenty-four-hour period, refrain from commenting on your children's appearance, criticizing their behavior, challenging their opinions, pointing out their shortcomings, telling them what to do, revealing their secrets, or feeling disappointed in them for not being perfect. If you don't have kids, try doing the same exercise with your partner or spouse. Refraining from emotional trespass will be almost, but not quite, as difficult, because you will never feel the emotional tug of war between your longing for closeness and your need for autonomy as intensely as you do with your parents—or reenact the conflict as relentlessly. How could it be otherwise, when you first felt that conflict in your family of origin—and still do, even if you think you're beyond all that by this time in your life?

More than likely you're not; the words may be different now, but the melody's still the same, and it's playing as background music in your closest adult relationships. Most people's intimate boundary style is the same with their partners as it is or was with their parents, because as adults we tend to seek out partners whose level of fusion and differentiation is the same as our own. If the boundaries in your family system were enmeshed (or overly differentiated), chances are they were in your partner's, too. And they will tend to be that way, only more so, in the family you two create together, unless you actively and intentionally interrupt what the psychologist Murray Bowen called the multigenerational transmission process, by which family boundary style is replicated in succeeding generations.

Here's another exercise: retake the intimate boundaries section of the Boundary Style Questionnaire (see page 55), only this time substitute the parent with whom you are or were most emotionally engaged for the lover or spouse you were thinking of when you completed it the first time. If you have children, take it a third time with them in mind. Chances are, all these scores will be within a point or two of one another. If they're not—if they're much higher or lower with your parents or kids than they are with your partner—it may be that your intimate boundary style has evolved in reaction to a childhood marked by extremely enmeshed or overly differentiated family boundaries, and what's going on today is what therapists call reaction formation—attempting to change the unacceptable to the acceptable. Reaction formation represses unconscious painful feelings or experiences by replacing them in conscious awareness with their opposite. As defenses against anxiety go, this isn't necessarily a bad one, but the danger is that the repressed emotion, now felt as anger or sadness, hovers in the unconscious, always threatening to break through and be enacted in the current relationship. In order to counteract the influence of the multigenerational transmission process, it's necessary (and sometimes painful or frightening) to bring it into your conscious awareness—to *have* it rather than *be it*, relate to it instead of being "owned" by or subject to it.

How Permeable Are Your Family Boundaries?

To get a close-up of your family boundary style, complete the following short questionnaire three times—once each for how you feel or act with your parents, your children, and your siblings. If you want to narrow the focus even more, complete additional questionnaires for each individual member of your extended family—mother, father, sibling, and child(ren).

Family Boundary Quiz

Read the statements and choices carefully before responding as some answers are different or are reverse-scored.

1. I worry or wonder about how open or private
   I am or should be with them. _____
   1 = never   2 = sometimes   3 = often   4 = always

2. I worry or wonder if they're keeping things
   from me that I ought to know. _____
   1 = never   2 = sometimes   3 = often   4 = always

3. Their moods and feelings affect my own. _____
   1 = never   2 = sometimes   3 = often   4 = always

4. I find it hard to stand up for my views and
   opinions with them.   _____
   1 = never   2 = sometimes   3 = often   4 = always

5. They are the same as they've always been—they
   haven't really changed, even though they're
   older now.   _____
   1 = not true   1 = somewhat true   3 = mostly true
   4 = very true

6. I think about cutting all ties to them and never
   seeing or talking to them again.   _____
   1 = never   2 = sometimes   3 = often   4 = always

7. When they say, "We need to talk," I feel anxious.   _____
   1 = never   2 = sometimes   3 = often   4 = always

8. There are things about myself I can't tell them.   _____
   1 = not true   1 = sometimes true   3 = often true
   4 = always true

9. Their needs take precedence over my own.   _____
   1 = never   2 = sometimes   3 = often   4 = always

10. I am not as emotionally close to or separate from
    them as I wish I were.   _____
    1 = not true   1 = sometimes true   3 = often true
    4 = always true

Total   _____

    Score this questionnaire the way you scored the one in chapter 3.
It should be pretty clear by now that the higher your score, the more
fused or enmeshed you are with your parents, siblings, or children;
the lower your score, the more differentiated or distant. A middling
score, between 20 and 30, is pretty typical, although if your children
are still under your care, your score with them will probably be significantly higher than with the other members of your family, which
is appropriate to your role as a parent. The last statement in this

questionnaire is the most telling of all; the other nine are the reasons why you answered the last one as you did and are a guide to where you need to focus your efforts in order to get what you're missing in the relationships they reference. Remember: you can only be responsible for what you do—for your part in the relationship. You're not responsible for the relationship itself.

If You Give Them an Inch, Will They Take a Mile?

Before you pass your faulty family-of-origin boundaries down to your kids, thereby ensuring the financial well-being of another generation of therapists, you have to accept the continued existence of that age-old conflict between wanting to be close and connected and also wanting to be separate and autonomous. You may realize that this conflict once defined your relationship with your parents but still be denying that it persists to this day, or labeling it as inappropriate, leftover business from your childhood. But that's just whistling in the dark—it's still there, and internally, at least, it's still affecting how you feel about your parents, if not how you deal with them.

You may think that "fixing" boundaries with your parents only means holding firm against continued or further invasions—about getting away from them, not getting closer to them. But since that primary conflict still colors what is essentially the most intimate relationship you will ever have, this strategy, which addresses only half the conundrum, won't work; in fact, it will make things worse. Because boundaries are more than a bulwark against emotional trespass; they are a process of interaction that's always seesawing between separation and togetherness, and if you put too much weight on one end of the seesaw, you'll upset what is sometimes a delicate balance.

A much more effective strategy—one that will get you all of what you want from your parents instead of just half of it—

is making as much of an effort to be close to them as you do in trying to be separate from them (or vice versa), actively seeking and
choosing the levels on which you can connect and communicate
with them, and the emotional atmosphere in which you can relate to
them authentically, lovingly, and equally, with the same amount of
energy you expend in maintaining enough distance to protect yourself from their emotional trespass.

"That seems pretty chancy," says Jenna, whose mother never
had an opinion, criticism, judgment, or piece of advice for her
daughter that she didn't force on Jenna, which she continues to do.
"Frankly, it's easier to run than fight . . . to avoid her rather than confront her. And if I give her any opening at all, she'll take it as an
invitation to walk all over me."

But boundaries aren't about controlling the other person—
they're about controlling yourself and your psychological "space."
While confrontation has its place in any relationship where
emotional trespass is the operative dynamic, that's not what
we're talking about here (although we'll get to it!). What we're
talking about is *engagement* with your parents, which assures
them (and reminds you) that you still love them, that you've
forgiven them their failings in the past, and that you not only
want but need them to be in your life in a positive and meaningful
way.

Because you do. We all do. Even the most offensive parents, the
ones who keep ignoring our No Trespassing signs, are still our parents and we're connected to them by ties of blood, history, and
mutual obligation we can't and shouldn't deny, if only because continuing to do so won't get us what we want and will sap our
emotional energy. Laurie's mother, who was an educator for thirty
years, was a strong proponent of "teachable moments," says her
daughter. "She'd see a child misbehaving in a grocery store and
deliver a lecture to the child's mother about how to handle it.
When we started driving, she'd clip out every story about an accident that involved teenagers and put it on the refrigerator. And, of

course, she never stops telling us how to lead our lives, even though we're all over thirty now!" After one of her most egregious boundary invasions, Laurie sat down with her mother. "I told her that the knowledge that there was someone out there to whom I was still vitally important, someone who was always thinking about me and worrying about my health, happiness, and welfare—someone whose baby I would always be—was the greatest gift a parent could give a child, and I was enormously grateful for it." Her mother was pleased by the compliment, and "after a hug and some tears," Laurie added these carefully rehearsed words: "So when you give me advice I haven't asked for, or tell me what you think I should have done or ought to do, or criticize my choices and decisions instead of asking me why I made them, it feels to me like I don't own that gift—you still do, and you'll take it back if I don't do what pleases you."

That's the kind of engagement I mean. It may take some effort, but until you find a way to love your parents *and* leave them, the areas where you can make real emotional connections with them and thereby experience at least a modicum of the closeness you will always need, you won't be able to achieve the separateness and autonomy you also crave.

Because they've been doing it for so long, it's not easy for most parents to break the habit of invading their kids' boundaries, no matter how old those children are—not even those enlightened ones who know they should. They may preface their remarks with, "I only say this because I love you," but that doesn't take the sting out of them, even if it's true—which it usually is. Of course, what you hear when they say this is the implied message in their words, which is *You're not perfect . . . yet*. That may not be what they mean— it may not even be what they say—but because it's how you felt when they said it to a much younger you and that meaning is still lodged in your emotional memory, it's how you still feel. And it's how you will continue to feel until you tell them as clearly as you need to that you want them to stop.

The Use and Misuse of Minimum
Essential Force

You may think you've already done that, not once but hundreds of times. But it's still possible that your parents don't recognize what they're doing, don't realize they shouldn't, or don't think it's such a terrible thing. After all, they're only doing it because they love you! So you have to do it again. And keep doing it every time it happens, repeating the same clear, unambiguous message, in the same neutral tone, without raising your voice, getting even angrier or more frustrated, or escalating a brush fire into a full-fledge inferno.

Here's a script you can follow: "When you (*criticize my housekeeping, tell me I'm putting on weight, complain to me about Daddy, ask me why I'm not married, and so on*), I feel (*ignored, disrespected, invaded, judged, treated like a child, and so on*). Please stop doing it."

This is a tremendously powerful statement. It's saying, *I want this degree of distance from you.* It's a good example of what the executive coach Peggy Gilmer calls "minimum essential force," which means just that—only what's necessary to get what you want. Anything stronger, and anything conveyed in a negative, critical, or demanding manner, especially if it starts with the words "You *always* do this!" is overkill. Anything weaker or more equivocal or ambivalent won't do the job.

But even minimum essential force won't work unless you combine it with another equally powerful statement that expresses in a positive fashion that you want closeness as much (well, maybe not quite, but let's not quibble here) as you want distance, the way Laurie did when she confronted her mother.

Kate's mother calls her at the office several times a day, usually to complain about Kate's father or brother or bemoan Kate's failure to commiserate with her about her problems or otherwise pay attention to her feelings. The phrase "I don't know what I did to deserve such a cold, distant daughter," or something similar, often finds its way into the conversation. Like everyone else in her family of origin,

Kate tries to placate her mother, apologizing for not paying enough attention to her and for putting her own needs and responsibilities first. It's a familiar and frustrating pattern, and it takes its toll on Kate's mood, her job, her time, and her energy, until she slams down the phone in annoyance, barks at her colleagues, and swallows a Xanax.

Kate had never actually told her mother clearly and unambiguously to stop calling her at work. When she finally did and also told her why—"When I'm interrupted at the office, I have to work later to make up the time, and I don't want to have to do that"—her mother still didn't heed her words. So she increased the force and added some consequences. "I've told my secretary to hold all my personal calls, so you won't be able to reach me at the office"—but the hoped-for respite was only a brief one. When it happened again, she tried adding these words: "Of course, if it's an emergency—if you or Daddy are sick or injured, for instance—I certainly want to know about it. Just leave a very specific message—tell my assistant or the operator that it's urgent, and I'll get back to you right away." That cut down her mother's calls somewhat, but only for a while— pretty soon, Kate's assistant was being treated to the same litany of complaints. So she sat down and had another talk with her mother. "When you involve my colleagues in our family business or discuss me with my assistant, it poisons my professional relationships, makes it harder for me to do my job, and causes me a lot of anger and frustration. It may also limit my future in this job, which I love. I want you to stop. If you don't, I'll instruct everyone in my department not to take your calls or messages, which will be embarrassing for you as well as them. More important, it will make it impossible for me to be available when you really need me."

Her mother finally heard Kate's words about calling her at the office, but she didn't stop trespassing on Kate's boundaries in other ways. Kate didn't give up—she continued to do three of the four things that you may have to do to establish your limit: name the specific invasion whenever it happens, describe how it makes you feel, and say what you want to happen ("You're talking about my weight again. It makes me feel unattractive, unheard, and disrespected. I want you to stop it.").

When that doesn't work, you may have to add more force—with your words, not with your tone of voice, body language, or expression of anger or frustration—and add the fourth step: establish the consequence. "I've asked you not to comment on my weight. I've told you how it makes me feel. I've asked you to stop. If you do it again, I'll (*hang up, leave, ask you to leave*)." Boundaries without consequences aren't limits—they're just nagging.

What finally made the difference in Kate's case, after she hung up a few times, was adding the carrot to the stick. When the phone rang in her office and she picked it up accidentally, or her assistant said her mother was calling again, Kate got the first word in. "I can't tie up the line with a personal call, but I've been missing you lately. Can we set up a time to catch up? I need a dress for Tom's office party and you're so good at bargain hunting—maybe we could go shopping Saturday morning. And then you can tell me all about it." Kate was consistent in the way she dealt with her mother's other emotional trespasses: what psychologists call "intermittent reinforcement" does more harm than good and rarely extinguishes negative behavior. When her mother made a snide comment about Kate's weight or the way she disciplined her kids, or told her what was wrong with her husband, Kate responded in a firm but loving way by putting the best possible spin on her mother's remarks. She gave her mother the benefit of the doubt but also made the effects of her remarks clear and established the consequences if she continued her trespasses: "I know that you're (*worried about my health, think I should be stricter with the children, are concerned about my marriage, and so on*). And I also know that you say these things because you love me. But this is my business, not yours, and no matter how often you say them, I'm not going to change until and unless I choose to. I think you should know that when you talk to me this way, it makes it very hard for me to show you the love I feel for you, too, or be as close to you or spend as much time with you as I'd like. This has been a problem between us for a long time. We need to solve it together. We could try a time-out until we come up with one, unless you have a better idea."

By expressing her desire for continued connection, clarifying how her mother's behavior got in the way of achieving it, framing it as a problem in the relationship rather than simply her mother's fault, offering to help find a solution, and even suggesting one herself, Kate eventually got everything she wanted—separation and connection—on terms she could live with.

How to Deal with Your Parents without Turning into Them

Chances are, if you're having trouble regulating distance and closeness with your parents (or siblings), it's nothing new. What's different is that as an adult, you're not as powerless as you once were. Now you can brandish what may seem like the ultimate weapon: emotional cutoff. But keeping your parents at a distance is still "keeping" them, at least psychologically. More to the point, it's ineffective; it provides neither real emotional distance nor meaningful connection.

Letting them trespass at will doesn't work, either, for the same reasons. And if you're still trapped in the faulty boundary style of your childhood—which you will be unless you transform it by acknowledging that you want and need both autonomy and intimacy and claiming your right to both by naming the trespass, speaking your emotional truth, establishing your limits, and connecting where and how you can—it's all but certain that with your own kids, you'll turn into the kind of parent you vowed you'd never be.

Do They Want the Same Things You Do?

It may come as a surprise to realize that your parents may not be any happier with your boundaries (or lack of them) than you are with theirs. While we're more apt to notice when they want more closeness than we do, we usually don't recognize when they need separation, too. This doesn't mean that they don't love us, any more than our need to claim our own psychological space means that we don't love them, either.

It's not surprising that one of the common side effects of reexamining the past—most typically as the result of doing it with a therapist—is the emotional trespass that results from dumping your resentments on your parents. But it's not their fault that your life hasn't turned out the way you wanted it to—and even if it is, at this point it's not their job to make you happy, if it ever was. And confusing the urge to share your problems with them with demanding or whining or blackmailing them into taking responsibility for them is trespassing on their boundaries, too. If what you need is something specific, ask for it (and be prepared to hear and accept no if that's their final answer). But if what you really want is just a sympathetic ear or a reassuring hug, make that clear before you share (as opposed to dump) your problems with them: "Mom, I just want to tell you that (*my marriage is in trouble, my kid is failing in school, my best friend is mad at me, I lost my job, and so on*). I'm doing the best I can under the circumstances, and right now I don't need anything from you except understanding that I'm going through a tough time" is more likely to get you that than some version of "My life is a mess, and I need you to fix it."

It's not just the less than noble desire for payback that sometimes leads us to treat our parents like children; it's a mixed bag of motivations that include our concern for them (especially as they age) as well as our need to demonstrate, even show off, how much smarter and more competent and/or experienced we are. But even if they've spent a lifetime invading our boundaries, doing the same thing to them isn't going to teach them a lesson, make them stop doing it, or improve the relationship—it will probably make it worse. Kristin criticizes the way her mother keeps house, treats her father, spends her money, and lets her friends take advantage of her; she nags her the same way her mother nagged her, with approximately the same effect—her mother simply ignores her. It wasn't Kristin who finally established her limits; it was her mother herself, who met Kristin at the door one day and said, "I'm glad to see you, but unless you stop telling me what to do, how to dress, when to wash the curtains, and why I shouldn't talk to Daddy the way I do, you can't come in."

Infantilizing your parents isn't the same thing as managing the inevitable role reversal that occurs when they can't take care of themselves; it's taking away their autonomy, not to mention their dignity. Respecting the boundary that exists between parents and children—no matter how old you or they are—is the only way to preserve theirs and safeguard your own.

Sibling "Boundage"

No, that word "boundage" isn't a typo; it's a description of what happens when siblings are locked into roles, identifications, and patterns of interaction established in their shared childhood that persist in, and plague, their adult relationships. "I'm the oldest, so I'm in charge." "They always loved you best." "You're still the diffi-cult one." "Why are you always picking on me?" "I'm not a baby!" "You're tearing this family apart." "Why do you always get (*the biggest piece, the seat next to the window, your own way, and so on*) and I never do?" "You don't care about anyone else in this family." "You're breaking their hearts."

Unless you're an only child, you probably heard or said some version of at least one of those phrases when you were growing up—and you're still hearing or saying them. If you are, it's likely that in the cast of characters in the family drama, you and your sibling(s) are still playing out, or playing into, the roles you were born or assigned to play: the pretty one, the smart one, the truth-teller, the liar, the rebel, the responsible one, the leader, the follower, the victim, the bully, the baby, the pleaser.

There were four girls in Stacy's family. "Mary was the helpless one—she tried, but she couldn't do anything right. Cleo was the oldest—she was a real control freak who told us all what to do. Val, who's the baby, was the rebel—she was always getting into trouble. And I was the mediator between my sisters and my parents." As Stacy tells it, those roles still characterize their relationships today. "Mary's got ADD, she's married to a difficult man, and her kids walk all over her. Cleo tells all of us what do to—still!—and gets mad when we ignore her. Val has this image of herself as totally independent, but when she needs something from our parents, she still goes through me to get it, which is how I got stuck with the lecture that was meant for her when she had to borrow money from our folks to keep her car from being repossessed—they said no at first, but when I pointed out that she'd lose her job if she didn't have transportation, they came up with it. And when I told Val that they said it was the last time they were going to bail her out, she just laughed."

In order for Stacy to establish adult boundaries with her siblings, she'd have to give up the role she's occupied in the family all her life and with it the emotional payoffs she derives from it: the secret satisfactions of one-upping Cleo ("She's the one who orders everyone around, but I'm the one who does what needs doing") and being the "mature one" her parents trust to speak to and for the others (and to whom they complain when Cleo tries to boss them, too). It would mean stepping out as the go-between in the family—especially for Val; encouraging Mary's efforts to take charge of her own life instead of enabling her passivity; and letting go of her old resentments against Cleo.

Establishing new adult boundaries with siblings isn't easy. It may take several attempts before they understand that you will no longer tolerate, or commit, the kind of emotional trespass that may have been a staple of family life once upon a time but isn't appropriate to your age, life stage, or relationship now. It may make you feel separate, distant, and even disloyal, and if your family boundaries were more enmeshed than differentiated, that's probably how you'll be perceived by your siblings, too. Focusing on what connects you rather than what divides you will mitigate that to some extent; so will making a real effort to resist their (or your own) tendencies to triangulate. Don't "interpret" or explain any of them to your siblings or to your parents. Stay out of the middle when it's not your problem, argument, or business. Keep out of their marriages, which aren't your business, and keep them out of yours. Let them raise their kids the way they want to. Allow them the privilege of having their own feelings about one another and your parents, even if you think they're wrong or misguided. Be the kind of sibling you always wished you had. And maybe—just maybe—they'll return the favor.

CHAPTER 6

The We of Me and Vice Versa

Long before we had words to express our needs, communicate our feelings, or explain our anxieties, there was someone who understood them. And ever since, we've been looking for an other who would do the same thing—know us better than we know ourselves and love us anyway. But despite the trace memory of that long-ago merger with a mother who seemed able to read our minds and anticipate our needs, the truth is that she never really could, and neither can anyone else; we can't know or be known more deeply than we know ourselves.

To find one's soul mate is a wondrous thing. But in love, what isn't consciously remembered is even more present than what's happening in the moment; the emotional memory of earlier intimate experiences is stimulated again, both our infantile fears of dependence and alienation and the contradictory strivings for connection and independence that we felt so consciously and passionately in adolescence. Intimacy embodies all the polarities of those earlier stages, as well as a unique paradox: the more able we are to let those we love into our inner world, engage with the reality of theirs, and risk being changed by the experience, the more intimate our relationships with them will be.

Our first experience with romantic love teaches us its

potential for banishing loneliness, but it also makes us aware of the possibility of losing our self: "Remember that play years ago, *For Colored Girls Who Have Considered Suicide When the Rainbow Is Enuf?*" asks Kayla. "The number that made a huge impression on me was the one with the woman whose lover had left—the refrain, which I've never forgotten, was, 'He almost walked off with my stuff.' I was twenty-four and head over heels in love for the first time, but by the end of that song all I could think about was everything I was about to give up for him—my apartment, my friends, even my job. He'd been transferred, and we were about to move across the country to a city where I'd never been and didn't know a soul—in fact, the movers were coming to take away my *actual* stuff the next day! I felt like if I went through with our plans, I would totally disappear! And as much as I loved him, I'd worked too hard to get a self and a life to let that happen." Kayla's inner boundaries are much more permeable than her intimate ones, which reflect both that first experience with love and the lesson she learned from it. "If I'd taken the intimate boundaries section of the Boundary Style Questionnaire back then, I would have answered it very differently," she says now. "In fact, I did that part of the questionnaire twice—as if I was still that naive twenty-four-year-old, and as I tend to act in intimate relationships now that I understand how much I need to safeguard my autonomy, even with the man who's now my husband."

The permeability of our inner boundaries affects how able we are to construct intimate ones, because intimacy is about letting our real self be known—not the "as-if" self, the false self, the pseudoself we may have developed in childhood to earn a parent's love or approval, or even the disguised self other people may want or need us to be, but our authentic warts-and-all self. "Sometimes I wonder if any man can ever deal with my neediness," says Tracy. "I try to disguise it by acting as though I want much more independence than I really do, but that doesn't work, either—most men see through it. I feel destined to go through life pretending to be someone I'm not, because that kind of desperateness drives people away."

It's not surprising that Tracy's boundary permeability is quite high and that her boundary flexibility is equally low; lonely for someone to fill up her empty spaces, she can't limit her openness even to those whose response to her desperation is critical and even toxic.

The Narcissistic Echo

In the children's story *The Velveteen Rabbit*, love made the toy rabbit real, but it's intimacy that makes people real to one another. Unlike the plaintive narcissistic echo that often passes for love but is really just a plea for someone to fill an empty place in us—*How do you love me, let me count the ways*—intimacy demands that we reveal ourselves in all our primitive, undefended glory, our inner as well as outer aspects, not only to a lover's unflinching (and perhaps critical) scrutiny but to our own as well. Says Jocelyn, "Being in love is like holding up a mirror to yourself; you don't always like what you see reflected back at you." It's no wonder that true intimacy is rare, since it often requires us to ignore confusing feelings, suppress disloyal desires, and repress conflicting needs. Even though women frequently complain that men don't open up about their emotions, it's often true, as Jocelyn says, that the only feelings we really want them to share are those that reassure us that we matter to them: "When was the last time you said 'Thank you for sharing' when a man said he felt trapped, or he needed more space, or even 'I don't think this is working'?" she asks.

Intimate boundaries allow two people to connect at what the psychoanalyst Darlene Ehrenberg calls the "intimate edge" in relatedness, the places where maximum closeness can occur without psychological trespass. Intimacy is built on trust—the expectation that we can leave our inner doors unlocked, as it were, without fearing that those we love will take advantage of their access to disparage or destroy our feelings, thoughts, and beliefs. We can only let someone in if we're confident that we can keep (or throw) him out if we need to; the best playgrounds have fences and a secure gate that one can open and close at will and lock if necessary.

Privacy and the Shelter of the Self

Intimate boundaries determine how much mutuality is possible in a relationship and whether we experience compromise and accommodation as losses or gains. "Sometimes it feels like we're playing a board game; you got this one, now it's my turn," says Diane, who's been married for two years. "I wish we were both better at trying to see the other person's point of view and not only understand but care about why he or she feels that way instead of just keeping score."

Privacy, territory, and self-disclosure are aspects of intimate boundaries that reflect how couples adapt their internal struggle to be both autonomous and connected. And how we experience our lover's claim to protect or regulate his or her own "space" in each of these areas is a real as well as symbolic expression of the state of our unions. "Sometimes I sit across from him at the dinner table and wonder what's going on in his head—whether he's thinking about replacing the storm windows or wishing he'd married someone else," says Vivica. "But when I ask him he just says, 'If you need to know, I'll tell you,' or 'Let's make a deal—you stay out of my head and I'll stay out of yours.'" Privacy and intimacy are often seen as conflicting rather than complementary needs, but they're not mutually incompatible. Since self-disclosure is an important element of an intimate relationship, many women believe that their lovers' emotional or actual withdrawal, preference for solitude, or reluctance to reveal their fears and vulnerabilities is at best an obstacle to intimacy and at worst an indication that they're unwilling or unable to make a real commitment to the relationship. Yet constructive privacy—what Donald Winnicott called the capacity to be alone—is in fact the foundation of intimacy; the complete elimination of personal boundaries and the denial of the importance of privacy produces only a pseudo-intimacy.

The ability to control and limit access to the self is as crucial to intimacy as openness; relationships don't follow an inexorable trajectory toward increasing intimacy, but cycle between periods of accessibility and inaccessibility, and the latter even more than the former often determines whether relationships escalate, stagnate, or deteriorate. Privacy within a relationship is a way of maintaining the integrity of the self; privacy outside it is a way of maintaining the integrity of the relationship. Rainer Maria Rilke's description of love as a state in which "two solitudes protect and border and salute each other" underscores the interdependence of privacy and intimacy, which aren't antithetical, but isolation, withdrawal, reserve, solitude, and concealment, which are all synonyms for privacy, have different meanings in intimate relationships.

"When he withdraws into himself, I know it's because he's working out something he's not clear on yet, and he's the kind of person who doesn't just shoot from the hip—he's got to have all his thoughts and reasons and facts lined up so he's not just steamrolled by my much more sort of ad hoc, off-the-top-of-my-head or right-from-my-gut feelings and reactions," says Gloria. "For example, when I found out I was pregnant, we were extremely close for a couple of days, but then he went real quiet on me. I thought it was because he really didn't want the baby. But he came home one day about a week later with these darling little baby clothes—a Green Bay Packers shirt if it's a boy and a little Packers sweater and pleated skirt if it's a girl. He told me again how thrilled he was, and then he said, 'I've been thinking about my job, and I want to quit.' Well, of course I went nuts—how could you do this now, we can't afford it, what will we do if you don't get another one, what about our health insurance, all that stuff. And he just listened and let me vent. But even in the midst of that, I knew he'd thought it all out carefully, he had his reasons, and he needed me to try to understand them. So when he started talking, I was ready to, which was easier because I knew he wanted the baby as much as I did, and he wasn't going to jeopardize that baby's future on a whim.

"Of course, I wished he'd have shared his feelings about the job, too, which didn't come out till later, when he got one he liked a lot better. Like, after he'd been there a week or so he said, 'I really feel like I can do well here—my boss isn't always putting me down the way Mel used to.' And then another time he told me he really liked the team he was working on and said, 'There was so much backbiting and jockeying for advantage at my other job I was always looking to see who was stabbing me in the back; with this team, I feel like we're all in it together, just like when I played ball.' So I have to sort of infer his emotions."

Gloria's inner boundaries are more permeable than her husband's; she's more apt to blend her thoughts, feelings, impulses, and sensations, while his tend to be more separate and distinct. Yet his boundaries in general are more flexible than hers are, which allow him to open himself up enough to take in and contain her anxiety as well as respond to it without letting her feelings overwhelm his reasoning.

Solitude and isolation have very different meanings in intimate relationships: "I respect Cameron's need to be alone sometimes, even though I don't have it as strongly as he does," says Sandra, whose intimate boundaries are more permeable than either her inner or interpersonal ones. "He'll go for a hike by himself for a day, or even to a movie alone, and he'll come back in a good mood. But isolation is a whole different thing. It's when he just seems to shut down entirely. It's like he withdraws from the world, even when he's here . . . as if there's this huge wall around him so nothing can get in or out. And then it'll be like presto! and he's back again." Once, after a few weeks of what Sandra calls "his retreat into the world of the living dead" she said, "It's nice having you back; where were you?" He just said, 'Fighting the good fight,' which I took to mean depression, which he's always struggled with."

Concealment usually has a negative connotation in intimate relationships. "It means someone's hiding something he doesn't want his partner to see or know and that he feels guilty or ashamed of," comments Patti. "There's something sneaky and underhanded about concealment—it's not the same thing as privacy, which has more of a sense of, This is something I reserve for myself, I keep to myself, it's not about us or you, it's about me."

How we perceive and label a situation as private influences our experience of it. If the antonym of private is exposed, then privacy as it touches the unknowable is fraught with danger; as it promises mutuality and sharing, it touches profound needs; and as it threatens exclusion, it raises fears. Boundary style colors how we feel about privacy—the more permeable our boundaries are, the more we need it, especially if we're not flexible enough to be able to limit that permeability to protect ourselves against taking in so much of the psychological surround that it overwhelms us, but it may also make us anxious and lonely.

What behaviors do partners conceal from each other, and why? What behaviors do they share? Does familiarity breed intimacy or contempt, boredom, disappointment, disillusionment, and divorce? Does he walk in and pee while she's in the shower? Does she read his mail or go through his wallet? Who makes the decisions, and about what? And who decides who's in and who's out of the relationship?

The Territorial Imperative

Shirley could never share a bathroom with her husband; it's not just that she wants to perform her bodily functions unseen or unheard, but it's the only door in her house that she can lock from the inside, which gives her at least a little control over her own surroundings, something she doesn't otherwise feel entitled to. Darlene used to use her five-mile run to recharge her batteries, connect with her own goals and priorities, and contemplate the state of her soul; even though she met James in a 10K race, she doesn't want his company or his commentary during her only private hour of the day. Joanne thinks that what she does with her own money is her business, especially after she pays her share of the household expenses; when Sean goes through her checkbook and inspects her credit card statements, she's furious. Susan can't bear it when her husband tells her how she's feeling or, worse, makes a judgment about it. Cassie's kids barge into her bedroom uninvited, but when she retreats from the fray and locks her door for a little much-needed time alone, ten-year-old Josie wails, "I hate it when you shut me out like that!" "I'm not shutting you out, I'm closing myself in," her mother responds, but to Josie it's the same thing: "I guess that depends which side of the door you're on," Josie says.

Territoriality is how people both prevent and react to the stresses and frustrations of living together. Implicitly or explicitly, we reserve, share, or even deed over certain areas of our physical and social space, from an amount of our personal time to the preferred side of the bed or the shelves in the medicine cabinet. Jan and Rob are independent people who both enjoyed being single; when they married in their forties, they decided to keep their own apartments, buy a place together in the country for weekends, and go on with their individual social and personal lives as they had before. "People say, what kind of a marriage is that, you spend more time apart than you do together," says Jan. "What I tell them is, it's a marriage that works for us." But even more conventional couples need what Erwin Goffman calls a "backstage region" for being alone, like Shirley's bathroom, or a symbol of separateness, like Darlene's solitary run.

Whose Full Disclosure?

Self-disclosure is almost synonymous with intimacy, but in some circumstances it creates distance in a relationship rather than narrowing it, either intentionally or inadvertently. While self-disclosure may promote intimacy, choosing not to disclose doesn't necessarily mean discouraging it; it may be an affirmation of the private self, a concern about the effect of the disclosure on the other person and/or the relationship, or anxiety or uncertainty about the response it might (or might not) elicit. Emily and Dan were married for over a decade when she told him about the child she bore and gave up for adoption at seventeen; to him, her long-delayed revelation signified a lack of trust in his love for her. "The fact that she kept it a secret for so long means she doesn't have any real sense of who I am. That's why I'm questioning everything now," he says.

Sharing private information, in effect, means that the discloser and the confidant co-own the revelation, because both are responsible for managing it. While lovers and spouses are expected to tell each other private thoughts and feelings, regulating the disclosure of private information—being selective in it rather than telling everything—may be a more successful strategy for relationships than practicing complete openness. Discretion, which leaves room for surprise as well as protecting vulnerabilities, may be important in preventing boredom from occurring in long-term relationships.

In some relationships receiving disclosive information is as risky as revealing it because the needs we meet by telling something private set up expectations for a certain kind of response from our partner. This demand-response dynamic goes on whether we disclose private information to express a thought or a feeling, clarify a position and have it acknowledged, gain compliance or agreement, confirm that we are valued and esteemed, or develop the relationship. If the last instance is our goal, we may implicitly expect that our partner will reciprocate with disclosures of his own, which will lead to further intimacy. But studies of how men and women communicate show that expectations are often not met because they are frequently not understood. When Zoe tells Eric about a problem she's having at work, she doesn't want him to solve it, she wants him to understand how she feels and empathize with it; as the author Deborah Tannen points out, men typically use conversation to report, women for rapport.

Over time, as expectations are met or violated, we develop ways to give and receive disclosive information strategically in order to minimize risk to the relationship as well as to protect our own vulnerabilities. "I've learned not to tell Tim when I'm mulling over a personal issue that he might construe as threatening to him or to the relationship," says Eve. "His initial response is always very narcissistic—he makes it a story about him, not me. Once I told him that a friend of ours was having an affair, and for weeks he interrogated me about whether I'd ever do that and told me if I did, he'd divorce me in a second. I had a cancer scare last year I never mentioned because I knew I'd have to take care of his fears and anxieties instead of dealing with my own." When she was a young adult, Eve had a drug problem, which she tried unsuccessfully to discuss with Tim when they became engaged. "I had been in recovery for several years before we got together, but his attitude toward drugs was so condemning that I never told him the full story. I still struggle with the impulse to use from time to time, but I can't tell him that; he'd never be able to give me what I need, which is reassurance that I won't relapse and appreciation for how hard I fight. Instead he'd lecture me about how it would destroy our relationship and make him doubt everything about me. It's the biggest secret I have from him; I hope someday I'll feel secure enough about myself and about him that I can tell him the truth instead of a prettied-up version of it." As her story indicates, a lie is a boundary that promotes distance, but in some cases it may be necessary to protect what intimacy already exists in a relationship.

Inside, Outside, and Around the Boundaries of Intimacy

Intimate boundaries reflect what's inside a relationship as well as what's outside it. The sociologists Wendy Williams and Michael Barnes conceptualized three kinds of couple boundaries in a model that's particularly useful in clarifying potential areas of satisfaction and dissatisfaction. The boundary around the internal world of the relationship itself contains all the partners' shared thoughts, feelings, and activities. While theoretically each person contributes to half of this world, many women feel that they do more of the "relationship maintenance" than their partners. Another boundary separates each person's own external world from his or her part of the internal world of the relationship. It should come as no surprise to women that relationships typically occupy a greater share of their inner lives than they do of men's. For men, the business of a relationship can seem like a distraction: "I love my wife, but it was a relief to get back to the office and concentrate on work again after the honeymoon," says Greg, who added that the only other time in his life that he felt as "unhinged," as he put it, was when his father died. Which underscores the findings of the sociologist Joseph Pleck, whose research indicates that male behavior is associated with seeking achievement and suppressing emotion; it's the latter that makes the former possible.

A third boundary between the external worlds of each partner indicates how separate or connected their careers, friends, interests, and outside activities are. Even two people who love each other may not appreciate that their partners' lives before meeting them contributed to who they are, and insisting that they jettison those important aspects of themselves on the way to the altar as a "loyalty test" of their new commitment is often a portent of future problems in the relationship. When Julie married Art, who had two children from a previous marriage, she extracted a promise that she and any children they had together would always come first—a promise he shouldn't have made and couldn't keep, especially when his former wife decamped and left the kids with Julie and Art. Treated as second-class citizens in their father's home, the frequent target of his wife's anger, the children eventually went to live with their grandparents and have refused to have anything to do with Art as long as he is married to Julie.

Suzanne's husband wouldn't let her have her own life. "First he made me stop the after-work drink with my office mates on Friday afternoons. If the phone rang after dinner and it was for me, he'd say I couldn't be disturbed or I didn't want to talk to them. Then he told me to quit the women's soccer team I've played on for years; our games are on Saturday mornings, which is when he likes to have sex. I had to leave him while there was still something left of me."

Welcome to My World and Please Stay Out of It

A couple's boundary style determines how they work out the overlap in their shared and separate worlds. Studies of love in close relationships indicate that while greater involvement in the relationship by men leads to satisfaction for women, greater involvement on the part of women does not lead to satisfaction for men. "I'm not asking that she sit in a duck blind for hours on a cold, wet fall day—I understand that's not her idea of fun," says David. "What I resent is her insistence on coming with me even though she hates it and then whining and complaining the whole time." "I know my wife doesn't 'get' Todd even though she doesn't say so," comments Marty. "But we've been buddies since high school, and I wish she could just accept that there's a bond between us that she's not part of and never will be instead of trying to push her way in between us." Paula can't abide her husband's continuing friendship with a law school classmate who happens to be female, even though there's nothing romantic between them and never has been. "It's as if I'm cut off from contact with any women except her," says John. "When we got married, I didn't realize that half the human race was going to be off limits to me, even on totally platonic terms."

Relationships work because of a balance between intimacy and independence, one that changes over time and influences changes in intimate boundaries, too. Gillian and her husband are lawyers in separate practices who often talk over their cases, offer each other advice, and socialize with friends who are also lawyers. But they rarely share their feelings with each other or discuss concerns they might have about their relationship. "I'm not that interested in my own inner life, or his, either, " she says. "There are times when we're pretty closed off from each other, when we're each wrestling with our own demons, but we just wait those times out. You know that old joke about the woman who keeps asking her husband if he loves her, until one day he looks up over his toast and eggs and says, 'As a matter of fact, I want a divorce'? One thing you learn as a lawyer is, don't ask a question unless you're absolutely sure of the answer."

How Close Is Too Close?

While boundary permeability permits greater emotional closeness in relationships, it doesn't necessarily mean more intimacy, or even a more satisfying and enduring relationship. Thicker intimate boundaries allow for less emotional interchange between partners, which may be why they're able to get along and live together without a great deal of conflict or drama, and it also underscores Hartmann's finding that married people tend to have less permeable boundaries than their single counterparts. "We stay out of each other's heads," says Gillian, "and we both like it that way." Communicating deeply, honestly, and intimately with a partner is not the only prerequisite for happiness; desiring to promote a lover's welfare, holding him or her in high regard, being able to count on each other in times of need, and having a mutual understanding are also important. But someone whose inner and intimate boundaries are significantly thinner might not find Gillian and her mate's relationship as satisfying as they do.

Problems ensue when there's not enough symmetry in a couple's intimate boundaries for them to feel understood by each other and reasonably confident that their emotional needs will be met.

Empirical investigations have shown that relationship adjustment is connected with indexes of boundaries between partners—how they function as a marital unit and how they function individually. A study of couples' standards and assumptions for and about their relationship showed that boundary similarity was one of the most significant dimensions in marital satisfaction; when both partners have similar conceptions about what constitutes a successful working relationship, it's more likely to work. Yet when two people fall in love, the boundaries between them seem to dissolve, minimizing at least temporarily the differences between what each needs and wants from the relationship, how much interchange there is between their inner and outer worlds, and how much of each person's life will be constituted by the relationship.

Some people choose partners who exhibit attributes they themselves wish they had or want to acquire. But often living with those partners is more difficult than they had anticipated; the conservative, closed-off, strong, silent man who falls in love with the sensitive, fragile, open, voluble free spirit is a convention of popular fiction, but in actuality, love exists within life, not outside it, and unless one is able and willing to change, the differences in their intimate boundaries may be too great to accommodate in their relationship. Anne, who's conservative and rule-abiding by nature and admits she wishes she were "less constricted emotionally" than she is, loved Josh's spontaneity, openness about his feelings, and especially his disdain of authority: "Secretly it thrilled me, the way the boys who were rebels in high school used to," she says. "I wanted to be one of them, except I didn't have the nerve." But after a while the difference in her values and boundaries and his began to bother her: "The rebel act wore thin. I realized his feelings were not only pretty immature—he was still blaming his parents for what they didn't give him—but also that because I don't spill mine out the way he does, he assumed I didn't have any. And living your whole life on the spur of the moment is exhausting—you never accomplish anything that way."

I and Thou

Intimacy is a continuing discovery of the uniqueness of the other, yet just as often what is revealed in a relationship is not what Martin Buber called the "Thou" but the "I." Creating our own version of another out of our wishes, desires, and fantasies, we miss the experience of a lover's authentic self; disavowing our conflicting demands for autonomy and connection, projecting our unacceptable impulses and contradictory feelings onto him, externalizing our own internal conflicts into the space between us, or reducing the other to no more than a missing aspect of our own wholeness limits the possibilities of truly knowing or being known.

Especially at the beginning, love thins and softens most of our boundaries, the inner ones even more than the outer ones. It revives emotional memories that have been buried in the unconscious, old conflicts that were never successfully mastered, and old needs that were never met. Sometimes the stimulated emotions are so powerful that the only way to keep them from overwhelming the self is by implicitly demanding that one's partner take them on, in a wordless exchange neither person realizes he or she is having; often old conflicts are reenacted in a disguised fashion in the new relationship. Depending on the strength of the projected needs or feelings and the permeability of the partner's intimate boundaries, he may respond with his own projections, which can be even harder to own or contain.

We choose and use our romantic partners to act out emotional dramas of which we're largely unaware. Krystal doesn't know where her hostile, aggressive feelings come from—she doesn't even know she has them, because Trey, who's inclined that way anyway, is willing to act them out for her, just as she's willing to take on his shameful (to him, anyway) vulnerability and his dependency needs; it's a game that only two can play, but both have to be willing.

The Spare Parts Swap Meet

Intimate relationships are to some extent an intra- as well as an inter-personal swap meet for disavowed, suppressed, or needed spare parts, aspects of the self we can't tolerate or desperately want. As long as both partners' inner boundaries are thick enough to protect them from being totally overwhelmed by the other's projected emotions and their intimate ones are permeable enough to express or enact them, their psychological needs can be contained by and accommodated within the relationship. But when one person refuses to accept what he intuitively knows isn't his—is, in fact, Not Me—the other has to take it back or act it out, either in the relationship or outside it. Not infrequently, we use each other to embody or restore a missing or needed part of our self. The dynamic may lead to a psychic plundering of each other's inner space: as the psychiatrist R. D. Laing wrote, "If one refuses collusion, one feels guilty for not being or becoming the embodiment of the complement demanded by the other for his identity. However, if one does succumb, one is seduced, becomes estranged from one's self, and is guilty of self betrayal."

The author Maggie Scarf describes the unconscious trading off of mutual projections and the role of projective identification in love and marriage as key to understanding conflict in a relationship. Inner boundaries influence the cocreation of intimate ones; they express the needs for autonomy and connection that are not only mirrored but magnified by the demands of the relationship. Projective identification can feel and look like intimacy, but the continuing flowing together of what is self and what is other erases an individual's inner boundaries and undermines what the sociologist Joseph Karpel called "the increasing definition of the I within the We," the process of differentiation that permits two people to nourish rather than plunder or trespass on each other's inner worlds. Intimacy holds out the tantalizing promise of solving the lifelong psychological dilemma of conflicting needs, which is why it's so appealing, but the less we can acknowledge those needs and experience them not as conflicts in the relationship but as integrated aspects of each other's individuality, the more elusive real intimacy will be.

Intimate boundaries are a process, which is why intimacy is also necessarily episodic; it may recur most reliably not when we seek it directly and continuously, but when we embrace it serendipitously. And while it's the foundation of love, it may paradoxically go away because of the threat it poses—the danger we start to feel to our existence as a separate, autonomous being. In the balancing act between intimacy and autonomy that goes on in every close relationship, a completely stable equilibrium is often never achieved. Yet without intimate boundaries that can accommodate that balancing act, both love and intimacy will be at risk.

CHAPTER 7

Where You End and
He (or She) Begins

How does intimacy survive the countless, casual boundary invasions and emotional trespasses that inevitably occur when two people become one couple? Trying to zero in on the differences between personal and marital boundaries, I asked ten couples who'd been together for at least five years to name the worst boundary violation they could think of, and this is what they told me.

Seven of the women said infidelity, and three of them added that that included emotional infidelity, as well as extramarital sex. One said, "Taking sides against me with the kids or other family members"; one said, "Embarrassing me in front of others"; and one replied, "Ignoring or discounting my feeling or opinions."

By contrast, while all of the men cited, "Telling other people about our sex life, especially her girlfriends," only three of the men said infidelity; asked about emotional infidelity, they replied, "If you mean having an itch but not scratching it, no." Said one man, "Telling someone things you don't tell your partner, feeling very close to them, really sharing at a deep, personal level, yeah, that would be infidelity even if there's no sex involved." Another described that as meaningless: "Is that one of those women's magazine things? Because it's very simple—either you're faithful to your vows or you're not."

What's Yours Is Mine and
What's Mine Is Mine, Too

A majority of men consider invading their physical, material, and/or personal privacy a violation of intimate as well as individual boundaries; among the most frequent examples of this they mentioned were, "Going through my pockets or personal stuff or listening to my phone calls"; "Telling people my private business"; "Wanting me to account for every dollar I spend"; and "Criticizing or embarrassing me in front of other people." "Bugging me about sharing my feelings" also made the list, as did "Eating from my plate, wearing my clothes, throwing out my things" and "Refusing to have sex unless she initiates it."

Except for infidelity, marital and personal boundaries are often confused or conflated. Part of establishing the couple bond is negotiating what's mine, yours, and ours; how much separateness each person claims (and the other respects) is different in every intimate relationship. Discussing any private aspect of your marriage with someone other than your partner without his or her consent is a violation of the couple boundary; invasions of anyone's privacy, including your spouse's, is a personal foul.

Living together in close quarters taxes both individual and couple boundaries—assuming that your partner's possessions (including his or her body) are the same as your own; attempting to control your mate's conduct, behavior, health, or appearance; and abdicating personal responsibility for your part in the relationship are routine trespasses that often fray the ties that bind. An even more common one is what Marjorie calls "the unfortunate habit of 'the Royal We,'" when one person in a couple speaks for both, often without the other's consent. "This is one of those seemingly harmless things my husband does that grates on me like nails on a blackboard; it makes me feel like I don't even exist except as an appendage of him," says Marjorie. And only extraordinary self-control and the fear of a long prison sentence has thus far kept her from reaching for a sharp object when Matt speaks for both of them: "It's as if my opinions and ideas don't even count," she fumes. "Did I give up my voice or the right to my own mind when I married him?"

The Boundaries of Money, Sex, and Power

What's shared and/or negotiated by a couple—what's inside the boundaries of the relationship—includes money, sex, communication, commitment, privacy, role responsibility, and management of the family system. "My mother used to say that she made all the unimportant decisions in the family, like whether to buy a house, where to send the kids to school, if they should join the country club. 'Your father takes care of all the important things, like whether both Chinas should be able to join the United Nations,'" comments Helena, who adds that when it comes to divvying up marital roles and domains, nothing is more telling than the difference between "taking care of the children, which is how women refer to being alone with their kids, and babysitting, which is how men view child-care responsibilities."

Many of what seem like marital boundary invasions aren't only that—they're an expression of an imbalance of power in the relationship. The emotional distance between two people increases when one has all or most of the power and the other has little or none; this is true of every adult relationship. And when the disenfranchised or disadvantaged partner tries to right that imbalance unilaterally—as Candace did when she moved the couple's joint savings account into one to which only she had access, "just to get his attention," as she put it; or as Carolyn did when she told Rick that she hadn't enjoyed sex since her pregnancy and wasn't interested in having it again; or as Lottie did when she told her stepson that he was no longer welcome in their home; or as Angie did when she said the same thing to her mother-in-law—the other partner experiences it as an invasion of his or her own boundaries as well as a rupture of their couple boundaries.

As the sociologist Pepper Schwartz points out, in marriage or long-term dyads, power tends to follow the money. The one who earns it often controls how it's spent, and the greater the financial disparity in a two-income family, the more power accrues to the greater earner. Sometimes the need to equalize financial power in a relationship takes the form of sexual withholding, adultery, or even addiction. Andy earned all the money and doled it out carefully to his stay-at-home wife, who only realized after her marriage was over that abusing drugs was her way of gaining some power in their relationship: "He didn't make me use—I did that," she said. "But there was a 'Gotcha!' element every time I did that I didn't realize until we separated, and it was gone, too; I didn't have that feeling around using any longer. I'm not blaming him, just stating a fact: being clean has been much easier since the divorce."

At least one person in every couple thinks making unilateral decisions without attempting to reach consensus first is a violation of the marital boundary, especially when the decisions affect the other person, their children, or their relationship itself. (And if that person isn't you, it's either because you're the one who's making them, or you feel powerless to assert your right to have a say, if not to get your way.)

When Lezlie had an abortion without talking it over with her longtime lover first, Grant was furious. "It may be your body, but it was our baby!" he told her. "That may be true, but ultimately it *is* my body," she countered. Their relationship never recovered from what Grant considered a major betrayal and she thought of as a decision she was entitled to make herself. "Knowing how much she didn't want a baby, eventually I might have come around to her way of thinking," he said sadly. "But the way she did it, without even telling me she was pregnant first—I felt like I could never trust her again."

Reproductive and sexual decisions are often where the rubber meets the road in terms of the personal versus the couple boundary. But so are other choices and behaviors that affect both partners and erode the lines couples draw around their relationship. Steve frequently invites guests to their weekend house in the country without consulting Penny, his wife. The fact that the guests are often business contacts or clients doesn't mollify her—in fact, it exacerbates her anger. "I feel as though it's a total violation of our life together. He works fifteen hours a day during the week, and this is time we agreed would be sacrosanct for our family. To give it away without asking me first is like putting our apartment on the market without talking it over, which he did last year. Or cashing in part of his 401(k) without telling me. Or keeping everything in his own name and having me sign our tax return without seeing it."

Boundary Crossers or Boundary Violations?

The difficulty with couple boundaries is that the only place they're spelled out is in the promises two people make when they marry or otherwise make a commitment to each other. Sexual fidelity is almost always agreed upon; so are those fuzzy concepts of "love, honor, and cherish," the poetic promises to promote each other's hopes, dreams, and aspirations, and the heartfelt vows to meet each other's needs. But many other behaviors that might seem like trespass to one spouse or partner hardly register with the other. These are "boundary crossers" rather than boundary violations. Another way of describing them is that they're only invasions if they feel that way to one member of a couple. In the context of your own marriage or intimate relationship, some of these acts might not even warrant discussion or consideration. But others may. And even if your partner has given up and stopped complaining about them, or never even mentioned how irritated, ignored, or intruded upon they make him feel, it's worth checking out whether they do. Because where the lines are drawn is a matter of opinion, and in a relationship, his opinion is as important as yours; if you've lost that loving feeling lately, and aren't quite sure where it went, it may be even more so.

So do this exercise with your spouse or lover. Check each of the behaviors on this list once if you think it's a marital or couple boundary and twice if you think it's a personal boundary. Put an X next to the ones your partner engages in occasionally or habitually. Ask him to do the same thing. And then discuss the results. You may be surprised to find that you have very different ideas about what's fair and what's foul in your relationship, your life, and your bureau drawer!

Couple Boundary Quiz

Going into your partner's purse or wallet _____

Using your partner's possessions without asking _____

Leaving the door open while using the bathroom or both using it at the same time _____

Making plans without consulting partner _____

Discussing marital relationship with outsiders _____

Interrupting partner's conversation _____

Disclosing information about partner to outsiders _____

Telling partner what (not) to eat, wear, or do _____

Criticizing partner's appearance _____

Sleeping separately _____

Vacationing separately _____

Restricting or being jealous of partner's friendships _____

Restricting contact with or criticizing partner's family _____

Making reproductive and contraceptive decisions
alone _____

Criticizing partner publicly _____

Criticizing partner privately _____

Controlling access to money _____

Reading partner's mail _____

Faking an orgasm _____

Making important personal or relationship decisions
unilaterally _____

Failing to communicate needs and feelings _____

Discounting or deriding partner's beliefs and/or
values _____

Labeling, explaining, or deriding partner's feelings _____

"Two People Together Is a Work Heroic in Its Ordinariness"

Adrienne Rich's words about first marriage are as true as those written a couple of centuries earlier by Ben Jonson, who called second marriage the "triumph of hope over experience." Regardless of which trip to the altar precedes it, any couple who manages to make an intimate commitment last—to keep love alive in spite of its ephemeral nature and to sustain faith in their relationship despite the daily assaults on it from within and without—has only done it because either or both partners are using their boundary intelligence, especially flexibility: "You have to be a little looser here, a little tighter there," says Marie. She bristled at Clark's habit of opening all the mail, regardless of whom it was addressed to; once she got her own computer password, and sole access to her private e-mail, it stopped bothering her. Charlotte hates it when Jerry asks her callers to identify themselves, so she has her friends phone her on her cell phone. Tammy doesn't get upset anymore when Warren complains that the house is messy or his shirts aren't ironed the way he likes them; she pays a maid out of her own money, and he picks up the tab for the French laundry that always remembers the starch.

But the marital or couple boundary is more than just a blend of two individual boundary styles—it's a whole other thing. It defines who's inside and who's outside, what the nature of the commitment is, what's shared and what's separate, how roles are allocated, and how conflict is managed.

Commitment—a Psychological Barrier Force

Most interpersonal connections, even close friendships, have no boundaries around the relationship, but those based on an intimate commitment to each other—especially marriage—are different. What one social scientist calls a "psychological barrier force" derives from two things: the internal obligations each person feels and experiences, and the outside constraints like legal, religious, family, and financial ties that inhibit walking out on the relationship when, as Marian puts it, "the tide goes out, and you don't believe it will ever come in again." Or, as Bonnie says, "When you get the idea you'd be happier somewhere else, and you just can't shake it."

When two people have different internal feelings about what commitment means, and different emotional experiences about it, the couple boundary is ambiguous. "It's as if there's a dotted line around us instead of a solid one," says Greta. It's not just about how open their inner worlds are to each other but also how committed each is, not just to the other person but to the relationship itself.

Mike and Maribeth have been married for five years, together for seven, and have a child together—yet there's something as tentative about their relationship as if they'd only just started cohabiting. "We got married when Sam was a year old, because of him more than anything else, and maybe because of that I've never been able to trust that he's as committed to us as I am," Maribeth says. "Mike never wanted to be tied down, even though Sam was planned, not an accident. He still acts as if he's single—I don't mean he screws around, he just makes decisions for himself without thinking about us, like buying a sports car instead of a station wagon, or spending more time with his buddies than he does with me and Sam, or quitting his job without considering that it meant losing our health insurance. I never know when he's coming home—he'll stop for a drink with his pals and call me at nine o'clock to say, Don't wait up. And he never comes to my parents' with me—he says he married me, not them."

Carla and George have been a sexually monogamous and emotionally intimate couple for a decade. But, still, she says, "Every week that passes and we're still together, I'm surprised. I know he loves me deeply and fully and is committed to me personally, but he's not necessarily committed to the relationship—at least, not as something you build a life on. I mean, he'll say, 'Sure, I'll still love you when I'm sixty-four.' But that's not the same thing as saying we'll still be together then—not to me, anyway. He has this thing about being free, at least philosophically . . . he still has a little studio downtown, although he's hardly ever there. And even though he pays half of all our expenses, he keeps the rest of his money separate." She adds, "I don't necessarily need to be married, not unless we had a child, but I do need to feel like our relationship is built on bedrock, not sand."

The Dance of Intimacy—One Step Forward, Two Steps Back

Samantha's description of her relationship with her husband underscores the different ways couples regulate distance. "It's like, the closer I get, the more Scott pulls away," she says. "So when he's too far away from me emotionally, I just pull back, which eventually brings him back. I used to think that was one of the benefits of marriage, as opposed to dating or even living together—that you didn't have to play those games, where someone's always the pursuer and the other one's the pursued. But now I just think it's in their DNA . . . the whole Mars and Venus thing." Although she's using her boundary intelligence to actively manage her permeability, she's doing the right thing for the wrong reasons—to control her husband rather than herself.

The sociologist Joseph Karpel found five different patterns in how couples regulate distance. One partner may distance himself or herself while the other draws closer, like Samantha and Scott. Or one partner may be the one who always seeks more distance, like George, who seems to feel an existential need to think of himself as free and unfettered even while remaining committed emotionally to Carla. Some twosomes alternate cycles of fusion and relatedness: "Sometimes we feel incredibly close to each other and other times we're like strangers inhabiting the same house," says Sylvia. But she echoes Marian's words and uses the same analogy about marriage: "The tide goes in and the tide goes out. That's just the way any long-term relationship is. I've had to learn a certain amount of patience, since his tides last longer than mine do! But I find that it always turns, and sometimes it even helps our relationship . . . it's like we get to discover each other all over again."

If the compromise between fusion and unrelatedness, or distance and closeness is an uneasy one, your relationship may be marked by continual conflict; when you can see the conflict as a difference in individual boundary styles, and you have a sufficient degree of boundary flexibility and enough complexity to find places to connect even when one of you is feeling emotionally distant, the conflict won't threaten the underlying stability of your relationship. "Whatever our fights seem to be about, they're really about one thing—one of us is feeling or being too separate from the other, and the other feels insecure personally and in our relationship," says Patricia. "When I'm wrapped up in a project at work, everything else gets shut out. Jeff will pick a fight about money, or complain about how the house looks, or get pissed off because I won't stop what I'm doing and go visit his mother in the nursing home. And then he'll say something like, 'Do you want a divorce? Because if that's really what's happening, just tell me and I'm out of here!'" She's learned to try to head off those times in ways that range from having sex even when she doesn't really want to—"Once I called him the day before a meeting I'd been focusing on for days and said, "Let's meet at home for a quickie, because I've got to work late tonight and it feels like forever since we've made love"—to putting notes in his briefcase that say things like "Have I told you lately that I love you?" or even sending him flowers at work. "It's a cliché, but it's true . . . little things do say a lot," she says. "What they say in this case is, I know I haven't been the world's best partner lately, but it has nothing to do with how I feel about you or about our relation-ship . . . those are solid, so don't worry."

The fifth pattern of regulating distance and closeness may seem as anachronistic as *The Stepford Wives*—at least, the original version. But "Big strong you and helpless little me"—or the converse, which is the basis of sitcoms from *Everybody Loves Raymond* to *Malcolm in the Mid-dle*, as in "Smart, strong, capable me and helpless, hapless, hasn't-got-a-clue you"—still reflects the reality of many marriages. However, when couples collude in this kind of charade by agreeing that one is mature and self-confident while the other is helpless and dependent, it's a setup for continued boundary invasions. Denise is a successful executive who manages a department of forty people and a budget of just under a million dollars. Yet she defers all important decisions at home to her husband—"Although if I really disagree, I have ways to manipulate him: last week when he wanted to refinance the house, which I thought was a bad idea, I said, 'I'm really glad you're so confident about the economy,' which I know he isn't, and later that night, after we had sex, I told him I was excited about all the things we could do with the money, like trade in the old station wagon, remodel the bathroom, and buy a time-share in Florida so we can spend more time with our folks. Of course, he doesn't want to do any of them—his excuse has always been, we can't afford it. By the next day, he'd decided that refinancing the house wasn't such a good idea after all."

The Ties That Strangle

Most couples don't regulate the distance between them according to one, static pattern; they move from one mode of relating to another over time as the context or the situation changes. And while avoiding conflict may seem like a way to maintain closeness, it also results in emotional distance. Behind the false front of togetherness that conceals underlying differences or minimizes the importance of disagreement—which is how couples work out compromises, achieve mutuality, and grow in their relationship—many partners in love and life move further away from each other as their individual needs are ignored or discounted.

Sharon and Mel act as if expressing, let alone acting on, their own desires for autonomy would threaten their marriage. They are determined to preserve the boundary of togetherness at all costs, but they both feel strangled by their relationship and wary of expressing their real feelings: "If I did, I'm afraid he'd question how strong my commitment to this relationship really is," Sharon says. Raised in enmeshed families with the message that dissolving or sacrificing the self is what marriage is all about, neither of them dares to challenge it; instead, they suffer and suffocate in silence, seemingly together, but actually all alone.

By contrast, Deborah and Stu's relationship is built on stronger ground because they've worked out a way to handle conflict that takes into account their different boundary styles. "I used to feel very vulnerable when we disagreed," says Deborah, whose boundaries are much more permeable than her husband's. "He didn't understand me; it wasn't just what it was about, that I wasn't really questioning whether he was right or wrong, but whether he loved me. I've had to really work at being open enough to hear his side of something without taking it personally. For instance, he gets annoyed when I don't enforce his rules for the kids, like doing their homework right after school or not letting them use the Net till their chores are done or get phone calls during dinner. I used to hear that as, 'You're a terrible parent.' But the truth is that I'm just a more casual one than he is; it doesn't matter that much to me if their rooms are tidy or they do their schoolwork before or after dinner. We've had to figure out what's important and what isn't . . . like, they can keep their rooms however they want to as long as they keep the door shut, but they have to clean up the parts of the house we all use. And they can do their homework whenever, unless their grades slip, in which case they do it his way. Together our boundaries sort of balance out . . . my casual ones and his more rigid ones."

That doesn't mean this couple never confronts conflict directly: "We pick and choose when to disagree," Deborah says. "And when we do, we stay with it until one of us convinces the other or we work out a compromise." It's a strategy John Gottman, an expert on conflict in marriage, calls "the validator adaptation," a more useful one than sweeping conflict under the rug or seeing every disagreement as a referendum on the relationship.

Watch What I Do, Not What I Say

Certain kinds of behavior by one or both partners in a relationship define or imply a weak, distant, or detached couple boundary that's vulnerable to distortion or intrusion by outer influences as well as degradation from within. Andy is often contemptuous, judgmental, and insulting to Nina—"It's not that he doesn't love me, it's just his personality," she says. "I don't even hear it anymore." Maybe not, but underneath her placid acceptance of his sarcasm and mockery is a simmering volcano that would consume everything in its path if it ever erupted. For Nina, withdrawal—not hearing—is the only boundary she has, because she can't be in a relationship with what she perceives as his failings. Kendra responds to her husband's need for approval, which she thinks is immature, by a kind of emotional cutoff, in which she exaggerates her need for independence and denies the importance of their relationship. "It seems like the more he wants me to tell him he's fine, he's smart, he's sexy, the less able I am to do it," she says. "It just feels icky to me; it diminishes my respect for him."

At certain moments in intimate life, relationship boundaries need to flex so either or both partners can reclaim their identities as separate human beings with their own thoughts, needs, and feelings—it's that eternal, archaic conflict between the needs for both autonomy and togetherness that's plagued every relationship since the first one with the first other. But when this kind of distance regulation is manifested by negative, reciprocal interaction—"Oh, you're moving further away from the relationship so I'll protect myself by cutting you off entirely," which is how Becky characterizes Marshall's reaction to her need for greater privacy and autonomy than her crowded home and "overload of coupleness" provides—even an otherwise strong relationship can dwindle into so much emotional distance that there's no way to reach across it and connect.

Connecting the Dotted Lines

When partners balance their needs for one kind of distance in a relationship by reaching out for greater closeness in another, the couple bond can survive and even flourish. For many couples, sex is the answer. "I can be a million miles away from him in my head, but as long as we make love on a regular basis, he doesn't seem to mind . . . he may even be happier that way," says Cathy, who touts passion's boundary-dissolving effect. "There are some couples who communicate their feelings through sex even if they can't talk about them or act them out any other way, and we're one of them. I don't know what would happen if we couldn't." For others, "refusing to take things personally" is how they cope with the fluctuations in individual needs for separateness. Stan lives in his own head a lot of the time—"Emotional intimacy is like Christmas—it happens maybe once a year," says Zandra. "Often I haven't got a clue about what he's thinking or feeling. But when he's sorted out whatever it is to his satisfaction, he can be really open with me. Meanwhile, I try to find other ways for us to be close. I'll start a project like painting the spare room and he'll say, maybe we should do the living room, too, and we end up doing it together. And then while he's doing the ceiling and I'm stripping the woodwork, he'll start talking about what's going on with him."

Sometimes it's difficult to believe that emotional distancing isn't necessarily a signal that there's trouble in the relationship. For almost a year after Dick's father died, says Mia, "he withdrew into himself . . . he was so unreachable I began to worry that he was going through one of those midlife crises that ends with a new Porsche, a new wife, and a new life without the old one." And the more frequently he attempted to reassure her by telling her it wasn't about them, it was about him, the more worried she became. "Finally I just stopped bugging him. I stopped focusing on *being* together and concentrated on *doing* together—in other words, I acted more like a man than a woman! I took up golf, which he'd always wanted me to do and I'd strenuously resisted. We took a vacation with two other couples, which took the burden off the two of us in terms of relating and also made us realize, if only by contrast, what a good marriage we have! We joined a gym together, and we even started a home-based business buying and selling on eBay—since I don't work outside the home, I did the lion's share of it, but he put in several hours a week, too, and we really had fun at it. We were a lot closer in many ways than we'd been in years, and when he finally did open up to me about how his father dying made him reexamine his whole life, and how hard that was on him—I mean, this is a man who never questions himself!—we moved to a whole different level of intimacy."

Francesca and Jeremy agreed from the beginning of their life together that if either of them had doubts or concerns about their relationship, they wouldn't wait till either or both had resolved them (especially not unilaterally) before they put them on the table, solicited each other's opinions and feelings about their differences, and worked out a way to proceed until the issue was settled. "I met a man at work to whom I was deeply attracted," Francesca said. "We had this flirtation that was terribly exciting to me, and the person I wanted to tell about it—Jeremy, who's my best friend—was the one who'd be most hurt by it. Even though I wasn't acting on it, and didn't think I would, I felt like I was cheating on Jeremy. So one night, after we'd made love and were feeling very close, I brought it up. I told him about Phillip—about how good it felt to have another man admire me, think I was cute and sexy, ask my opinions, send me funny e-mails, and shower me with compliments. I also told Jeremy I had no intentions of going any further with it, that this relationship had nothing to do with him, but that it made me feel young and alive, and I didn't want to give it up. Sexual fidelity is a given between us—if either one of us had an affair, I think it would destroy our marriage. But because I didn't have to keep my crush on this other man a secret, I think it actually helped it. And it sure made a difference in how Jeremy treated me, too!"

Different ideas about what constitutes an intimate boundary don't have to weaken a marriage—sometimes they can strengthen it, especially when you bring them out in the open instead of ignoring them. When Brett wondered aloud if he was just too solitary and self-involved to be married, Lena didn't panic. "I told him I had those doubts, too, but so far the positives outweighed the negatives. I also told him that I needed to do certain things to cope with his uncertainty, like go back to school and get certified as a teacher so I wouldn't feel so financially dependent on him and make some friends on my own so I had some close relationships outside our marriage—not sexual, but not all with women, either. I went on a meditation retreat by myself and came out of it feeling sure that whatever happened, I'd survive, and I also went on a diet, just in case I had to put myself back on the market! All those things were to strengthen me, not punish him for his uncertainty. And in the end, they reaffirmed us as a couple, too—maybe it was him getting a taste of my independence needs as well as his own."

Two different boundary styles strengthen a relationship rather than weaken it when you can reach across the distance created by your differences to create an intimate boundary that's not blurred by pseudomutuality and collusion. Trying to fit together at the expense of individual differentiation denies the need for separateness even (and especially) in marriage and avoids the anxiety of aloneness. There's no getting around the fact that some individual needs and desires may find few expressions in marriage; even in the best relationship in the world, there are times when one is the loneliest number.

Who's In, Who's Out, and Who's Counting?

Of course, there are also times when the couple boundary is stretched beyond reasonable limits and loneliness isn't the problem—interference is. As the psychiatrist and researcher Pauline Boss points out, boundary ambiguity is one of the biggest fault lines in a marriage. When there's little clarity or a lack of agreement between partners about who's inside the family system, when they're there, and what their roles are, the definition of couple or family is clouded by uncertainty.

It's not just the stuff of comic strips and sitcoms—sometimes it's competing loyalties to your own family and your relationship that challenge your marital boundaries. Clare seems more present and emotionally available to her father than to her husband. She was always the favorite daughter, the one who won the competition with her mother for his affections, and no man has ever surpassed him in hers—not even her husband, Jim. "She'll drop whatever she's doing if he calls, no matter what other plans we've made. She even answers the phone if he calls while we're having sex—how weird is *that*? I won't let her take money from him, but he bought her a new car last year, and she said she wouldn't hurt his feelings by refusing it. He criticizes the way I am with my boys even though he was a lousy father himself—none of Clare's brothers will have anything to do with him," Jim says bitterly.

Of course, it's hard to know how much anger at his own father Jim is displacing onto his father-in-law, since he's just as emotionally enmeshed with his father as his wife is with hers, although it takes a very different form; he's cut his dad off emotionally and has as little to do with him as possible. "Jim has never forgiven his father for walking out on them when he was a kid. Even though his dad is old and sick and dying now, Jim can't let bygones be bygones. His anger and hatred toward his father take up all the space in his heart and our life . . . sometimes it feels like there's no room left for me," says Clare.

Freud said there are always six people in the marital bed—the couple and their parents. Clare and Jim are an extreme example of this dynamic, but at certain times in the life cycle, the emotional and physical pull of their childhood families stresses every couple—they don't call it the sandwich generation for nothing! Maintaining the clarity of the couple boundary when parents are divorcing, remarrying, aging, ailing, and dying isn't easy— sometimes it feels like there just isn't enough emotional energy, space, and time to go around. "As much as I sometimes resent how close Ted is to his mother, especially since it cuts into our personal time, it has its positive sides, too," says Joan. "First of all, I truly love Georgia . . . if she weren't as wonderful a person as she is, I might feel differently. They have a special bond, maybe because she brought him up alone, and I have to respect that because I know how tough it was for her. Second, he doesn't compare me to her—not to my face, anyway—if he did that, I'd kill him! Third, I think the way he cares for her sets a good example for our kids, even though sometimes they complain that he spends more time with her than he does with us. But then there are those occasions when I feel like a third wheel in my own marriage, especially when she gets in the middle and Ted doesn't tell her to butt out. She gets her say in every discussion or decision we make, whether it's about buying a new house or disciplining the kids. Frankly, it's the biggest strain on our marriage. But the bottom line is, she won't be here forever, and I will!"

The couple boundary can't always hold out against other forces when one person is physically present but chronically absent psychologically. This often happens when both people are doing their own thing, not communicating their feelings or sharing their experiences, and filling up their leisure time with social activities that don't do much to reinforce intimacy even if on the outside, at least, it appears to strengthen their identification as a couple. Like Penny, who complained that even when her husband was alone with her in their country house, "his mind and his energy were somewhere else, focused on a business deal," the partner of such a spouse feels neither single nor married, constricted by loyalty to the marriage from finding emotional intimacy elsewhere. For Donna, as for many women, a close circle of female friends sometimes fills this void—"They drain off some of the loneliness," she says. Josie has a range of somatic symptoms that reflect her internal struggle between her need for intimacy and her fear that it will consume her—it's not surprising that many of these real, not psychosomatic, illnesses are autoimmune conditions. That they also provide her with a close connection to her health-care providers, who don't require reciprocal attention to their own needs, isn't particularly surprising given her boundary style, which is both highly permeable and low in complexity and flexibility.

Some people cope with their partner's psychological absence by filling up that empty space with affairs, careers, and triangulated family boundaries with their children. And still others, acknowledging the impossibility of finding any fulfillment inside such a one-sided couple boundary, cut and grieve their losses and move on.

When couples aren't clear about their roles, rules, and responsibilities in the relationship and in the family, and when either partner doesn't perceive them as satisfying, the couple boundary is always under siege. Despite the age-old arguments about who takes out the garbage, who disciplines the children, who earns and spends the money, how career and family responsibilities are parceled out between partners, and how the big-ticket choices and major decisions are made, if both people agree on the parameters of their individual and joint domains and think the power in their relationship is evenly balanced and the roles each inhabits are fair and appropriate, the boundary around the relationship can accommodate the ups and downs of intimate life, including the exits and entrances that characterize families across the life span. The points of maximum closeness where two people can connect without violating each other's personal boundaries are different in every relationship. But finding that often elusive intimate edge, where the tension between their individual needs for togetherness and solitude are balanced enough to afford both partners enough of each to accommodate the differences in their personal boundaries and create an intimate one that complements rather than conflicts with them, is the real challenge for every couple.

Couple Boundary Do's and Don't's

Every couple has to decide who's in and who's out of the marriage, so loyalties and priorities are clear. You may have to clarify it pretty directly—"Your mother has a place in your life, but it's not in the middle between us," or "Even though we're not married any longer, we're both still their parents and we need to act as a team with the children and not jockey for advantage or use them to fight our battles."

Similarly, both you and your partner have the right to set limits and establish boundaries to protect yourself, but not to control or change the other person. Establishing consequences matters as much to the success of boundary setting in marriage as it does in every relationship. While those consequences should be serious enough to matter, making them so severe that they become the problem—like dealing with a mate's power grab over the joint checkbook by maxing out the credit cards, for example—just substitutes one invasion for another.

Boundaries shouldn't be an ultimatum in your intimate relationship; considering them as a way to heighten the awareness of the duality of your feelings about independence and connectedness and get comfortable with them instead of running away from them is using your boundary intelligence to achieve enough of both to keep intimacy nourishing your individuality instead of suffocating it.

Ex-Laws and Outlaws

It's easier to shed a spouse than to create a new relationship with him once the ink is dry on the divorce decree—both the relationship in your mind, which lingers long after the formalities are over, and the one in the real world. Because more than your roles, responsibilities, address, or lifestyles are different—so are the boundaries between you. And most of the problems that two people have who used to be married (or some version thereof) and now aren't come from not recognizing, remembering, or accepting that.

Chris still treats the house he and Drindi used to live in together—which she now owns—as his own, "in a million little ways. Like walking in without knocking, opening the refrigerator and helping himself to what's inside when he picks up the kids or drops them off, or looking through the mail if it's on the front table. I hate it and have asked him to stop, but he still does those kind of things," says Drindi (What he also does is put the storm windows on, fix the garbage disposal, and clean the gutters, but she hasn't asked him to stop doing them; in fact, there's still a "honey-do" list on the refrigerator where she always kept it, and she updates it regularly.) Melissa touts her triumphs to Jay—especially her social and sexual ones; he in turn tells her that she needs to lose weight, their old friends never liked her, and she's turned into her mother the way he always knew she would. Sydney broods about who her ex-husband is seeing and uses their kids to find out. Sheila unloads her anger, sadness, and depression on her former husband and their college-age daughter. Gay asks her ex's secretary personal things about him that are none of her business. And Holly rings her ex for a booty call whenever she wants sex.

These aren't just old habits that are harder to break than his mother's china, which you never liked but nonetheless insisted on taking in the divorce settlement—they're emotional (and in some cases, physical) trespasses. They can make a good divorce (and yes, there are such things) go bad, destroy what positive feelings still exist between you, and postpone the moment when you realize that it's truly, truly over.

While it's true that two people who had children together will share a lifetime bond—and mutual love and responsibility for them—it's also true that you're not parenting them together anymore, at least not on a day-to-day basis, and you have to create new boundaries that reflect that. You need to know what you can control and what you can't, even if it affects your kids—including, in most cases, his postdivorce sexual and romantic relationships, his lifestyle in general, the rules he enforces and those he doesn't, and the way he spends time when they're with him.

You shouldn't have to be told that using your kids to keep an eye on your ex is a bad idea. Or that involving them in any of the details of your breakup, bad-mouthing their father to them, or making them bear the emotional brunt of your feelings about him are even worse ideas. Your boundary intelligence is what's called for here—especially awareness. Insight may take a little longer—analyzing the trespasses (yours or his) and figuring out what they really mean. Are they an effort to hold onto the past or to let it go? Are they related to old business that was never really resolved, or an effort to demonstrate, as the old ballad has it, that "I get along without you very well"? Only then can you commit to a strategy that clears up the ambivalent messages you're getting and giving and take action to manage your boundaries in a way that can transform your relationship with your ex and move it onto a different level.

That's not only useful when you have kids together—it's essential. Because he's the one person who has the same emotional and biological investment in those kids that you do and loves them just as much. When they need their parents—and when you need them—to celebrate joyous occasions or help them through hard ones, two is always better than one.

Kelly has been married twice and managed to keep both her exes as friends—the husband she married at twenty-five and divorced five years later gave her away when she married her second, with whom she shared two children and two decades together. Both have new families, who spend Thanksgiving together. "We liked each other enough to marry, and we shared important parts of our lives. Just because the passion dies, there's no reason for the friendship to go, too."

Of course, there are important differences between friendship and intimacy, and different boundaries define them. In the next two chapters we'll look at what the research can teach us about friendship and how using boundary intelligence can make yours better.

CHAPTER 8

Social Bonds and Boundaries

Faith says she could do without a lover, but she'd be lost without her friends. Lee says there are people she'd ask for a ride or a loan or a reference but only a couple she could phone at three in the morning. Ten-year-old Jadyn says she'd rather be her mother's friend than her daughter; friends are nicer to each other than parents and children, she says, because they have to be.

Love completes us—it supplies what we need and offsets what we lack. Friendship connects us—it's our link to other people, to the community of familiar strangers, acquaintances, chums, comrades, and colleagues who make up what the psychotherapist Marvin Thomas calls the personal village. Although the absence of either kind of relationship causes loneliness, one area of satisfaction can't substitute for the other—it's the difference between community and attachment. The qualities we seek in our friends aren't necessarily the same ones we desire in our most intimate relationships. For one thing, friendship doesn't require the limbic resonance, the feeling that our emotional brains are in harmony with one another—also known as the two-hearts-beating-as-one effect—that intimacy promotes.

Interpersonal boundaries are about social contact rather than psychological connection; they protect our personal integrity and wholeness without triggering anxiety about losing the self. Friendship in all its infinite varieties strengthens our sense of self; we believe in ourselves more when other people share our same experience, validating our common humanity as well as our individuality. Being seen, heard, and known or even just recognized confirms that we do, indeed, exist. As Faith says, "On a day when you're feeling low, a smile from the barista who doesn't know your name but knows how you like your coffee and starts making it that way when she sees you come in, or a compliment on your new haircut from the conductor on the commuter train, can make all the difference in how you feel." And not only that—according to Marvin Thomas, the personal village is a place to find privacy and escape from the mind-numbing stimulation of modern life without withdrawing entirely from it—those interactions that provide a sense of belonging or recognition without demanding any effort on our part are essential to our mental health.

How we relate to people in the personal village depends to some extent on our inner boundaries; generally we find them in or project them onto the world. Interpersonal boundaries reflect us, while intimate ones complement us—that's why opposites often attract in love but less frequently in friendship, where symmetry matters more than complementarity. Interpersonal boundaries are closely related to personality traits, which tend to be stable over time—generally, the more permeable these boundaries are, the more extroverted, open, and gregarious we tend to be. But flexibility is as important as permeability in determining how close or distant we are to others and under what conditions.

Bree is a warm, vivacious woman who reaches out to everyone she meets—it's as natural to her as breathing. And most people respond to her overtures of friendship. But when someone doesn't, she's deeply hurt; her boundaries are stuck in the "open" position. So are Mandy's; she can't close them down enough to protect herself from her supervisor's criticism, her best friend's depression, or the judgments (real or imagined) of people she barely knows, like the salesgirl at Bendel's who looks her up and down and says, 'I'm afraid we don't carry anything in your size.'"

The boundaries that connect and separate us from other people are more fluid than inner or intimate ones because they're dependent on context, role, and situation. They change not only according to how close or distant we want to be to someone at a particular time but also on the external cues we pick up about how welcome we are. The boundaries also depend on the social rules that structure the encounter; what's appropriate at one time, in one place, might be quite different from what goes in another situation, as anyone knows who's ever made a fool of herself at the office Christmas party or run into her shrink at the opera.

The Social Exchange Theory, or What's in It for Me?

What do we get from relationships besides relief from the existential loneliness of the human condition? The social exchange theory posits that relationships are entered into and sustained by the exchange of resources: money, goods, time, love, sex, validation, opportunity, or other material or personal payoffs. As in economics, from which this theory is derived, human interactions depend on the balance of costs and reward. The likeliness of developing a relationship with someone is based on the perceived possible outcomes—both the intrinsic ones, which are those that make us feel better or happier, and the extrinsic ones that satisfy a social or a material need. When the outcomes are perceived to be greater than the costs, we move closer toward someone and disclose more of ourselves; if the opposite outcome is more likely, we usually opt for greater distance.

But who's counting? As a matter of fact, most people are. Parity matters more to Amelia, who always remembers whose turn it is to call, drive, or pay and calibrates to the erg the amount of energy she expends in every relationship, than it does to Annette, who believes that even if what you give doesn't always equal what you get, quality counts more than quantity, and karma catches up with everyone eventually. But even Annette notices when she keeps getting the fuzzy end of the lollipop from certain people, although she's more likely to move back a few steps in those relationships rather than break them off completely, to keep them at a distance rather than confront them about the inequalities in their friendship.

The more complex the interaction or boundary process, the more complexity and differentiation it draws out of us and the more parts of the self we bring to the relationship. With a familiar stranger—the checker in the grocery store, the teller in the bank—we offer and receive little more than an acknowledgment of our mutual existence. With a close but not intimate friend—the woman in the book club who shares our taste in nineteenth-century novels but not our politics, the coworker with whom we go running at lunch, the guy we met on jury duty, the couple we share a ski house with every winter—we bring more of ourselves to the space between us, carefully edited bits of our personal history, our likes and dislikes, our habits of mind, and some of our feelings (although usually not those that signal our deepest fears and insecurities).

Social intimacy grows when and if we let more of others into our inner space and that movement is reciprocated; if it isn't, we pull back, sometimes so embarrassed by our disclosures and their silence that we end up apologizing for them. When our boundaries are complex enough so that we can appreciate but not be overcome by the differences between ourselves and others, our feelings and desires don't need to match with theirs in order to preserve our self-coherence. For instance, we can comfortably tolerate a discrepancy between what someone wants, expects, or needs from us and what we feel capable of giving; we're able to consider our own needs and those of others independently because we're differentiated enough to manage our feelings on our own.

Merging or Submerging?

Ask most women who they are and the top three answers they give will probably refer to their relationships—wife, mother, daughter. But being defined by these relationships makes it almost impossible to distinguish our sense of self from others' sense of us—that is, to recognize and, if necessary, deflect their psychological influence. At what Robert Kegan calls the interpersonal stage of mental growth, we experience those influences not as distinct parts of us or voices within us but as the whole of us, which means that how others experience us makes us who we are.

Intimate boundaries are a process of negotiating psychological closeness, while interpersonal ones have more to do with negotiating physical and mental distance and limiting the psychological influence others have on us. The more complex our processes of distinguishing Me from Not Me, the more safely we can reach out to others without risking harm to our deepest self.

The increasing complexity of the boundary between self and other has been demonstrated to be a stage-specific indication of psychological growth. Kegan, a Harvard professor and a key figure in the constructive developmental school of psychology based on theories of mental growth described earlier by Jean Piaget, calls the earliest stage of development incorporative—there is only a minimal differentiation between self and other, a barely felt boundary between the infant and his or her surroundings. At the second, or impulsive, stage, the self is embedded in and subject to its impulses and perceptions; like the toddler in the high chair in an earlier chapter, we don't *have* impulses and perceptions, we *are* them. In the imperial stage that ushers in childhood, we can distinguish the difference between our physical and mental state and other people's. Beginning to be aware of rules, roles, and the external others who embody them, we can not only recognize but even manipulate and make use of other people's thoughts and feelings to achieve our own goals. We know, for instance, that if we complain that we're tired, we can get out of putting our toys away, and that if we cry when we fall, Mommy will pick us up or even give us a cookie. But we're not yet capable of abstract thought and we can't internally coordinate more than one viewpoint.

The interpersonal self identifies with what it internalizes; at this stage, which begins in early adolescence, we take in others' thoughts and feelings psychologically as the sources of who and what we are. We still can't construct, define, or experience our self independently or prioritize among competing expectations and loyalties. This is when boundary invasion and emotional trespass first become real to us, and even the most casual intrusion threatens our sense of personal integrity. Defined by our relationships, we take personally whatever happens in them; we experience the trespass or the violation as an assault on our very essence because our relationships—even our most casual ones—are who we are.

At some further point in our psychological development (which is not necessarily tied to a chronological age or a life stage, according to Kegan's model), the interpersonal stage may be succeeded by the institutional stage. This is a more complex, differentiated level of self-construction; instead of *being* our relationships, roles, internalizations, and identifications, we have and manage them. In other words, we are the administrators of the self—as April says, "I run my own committee now instead of letting it run me." At this stage, our boundaries are complex enough to protect us from being taken over by either an internal voice or an external influence—no single member of our "committee, " no role or identity or part of the self predominates, and no interpersonal relationship generates or controls our feelings and behavior (at least, not for long).

Eventually we may arrive at the stage of psychological actualization where defending and maintaining psychological boundaries becomes relatively unimportant, because in all our relationships we are able to distinguish not only the parts of our self but the parts of other people. So every choice we make becomes a boundary, a process of relating part-to-part, or aspect-to-aspect. Says Chandra, "I've gotten to where I can listen to my closest friend tell me about her conversion experience without having it make me wonder about my own spirituality or comparing it to hers. I can find common ground in how concerned we both are about our children without dwelling on the huge difference in how we discipline them. I can even appreciate the happiness she feels in her much more traditional marriage than mine without wondering how she stands her jerk of a husband!"

In short, we can choose the levels on which we connect with others and those we don't; we can have different friends for different reasons, open ourselves to certain aspects of people while closing ourselves off to others, and define ourselves and all our relationships by what we want or need at any given moment in them. "Where before there was a self who ran the organization, there is now a self who is the organization," writes Kegan. "Having no need to defend a particular self-system that I am, boundaries take on a whole new level of relative nonimportance . . . not that they become useless or nonexistent, but that they are revitalized to create a different kind of relationship between things or people or parts of my self, to create a different kind of dynamics with other people or change the direction of an interaction. The process becomes the end rather than the means to an end."

Between the end of one stage of development and the beginning of the next is a midpoint Kegan calls an "evolutionary truce," when the ways of organizing our psychological experience begin to change, and so do our minds themselves, transforming the very structure of the way we know. The movement from the interpersonal to the institutional, from one order of awareness to another, affects all our relationships, at least internally and usually externally, too. It isn't that they no longer matter to us, but they matter in a more incremental, less global way; they're not us any longer—at least, not all of us—and we are not all or only them.

Why Boundaries Are Like Quantum Physics

Until neuroscience develops the tools that enable us to actually see boundaries, we can only infer things about them by looking at the variety of our relationships and the way we make sense of them—how we understand the experience of closeness and separateness, what it feels like when boundaries fit and when they don't. Nancy Popp writes, "As with quantum physics, the closer we look at the nature of boundaries, the more we see that there is really nothing there *but* energy, or the interaction of energy."

It's that energy—the movement between the two modes of relatedness—that at any given time defines exactly where, why, and how we change our boundaries and move closer to or farther away from others. This depends on many things—how long we've known someone, how much we've exposed ourselves and risked being vulnerable, the kind of conflicts and confrontations we have, what we have in common, the balance of reciprocity and equality in our relationship, whether we feel known and understood, the cues we get about whether we're welcome or wanted, how able we are to hold our position in the face of their opposition, and how much responsibility each of us takes for maintaining the relationship.

The Rules of Engagement

Some relationships come with an agreed-upon set of boundaries, implicit and explicit rules of engagement that define the appropriate distance between teacher and student, doctor and patient, employee and manager, for example. Others are defined by place—home, work, the playing field, the public space, the private table, the common ground. And still others are determined by the roles we and they play in others' lives—parent, child, lover, colleague, teammate, confidante, close friend, or casual acquaintance. Many depend on time and/or circumstance, particularly those the writer Judith Viorst calls convenience friends, whose lives routinely intersect with ours. They are neighbors or acquaintances with whom we've built up what Marvin Thomas calls social capital, a fund of reciprocity that we can draw on when we need to or offer when they do, whether it's driving the kids to soccer when we're sick or watering their plants when they're on vacation. We don't tell them too much or come too close; with convenience friends we maintain our public face and reveal little of our deeper emotions.

Historical friends, by contrast, are those with whom we once shared more intimate relationships but who've drifted out of our orbit today; the college roommate, the woman we met in Lamaze class, the friend we long ago cycled through Europe with. Like crossroads friends, we meant a lot to each other at some point in our lives, and even if we seem to have little in common with them today, they still have a permanent place in our personal village. And there are also those people with whom we have a common purpose, concern, or interest—affiliates rather than friends, others with whom we don't share our inner lives but do relate to on some common ground, whether it's a church fellowship, Weight Watchers, the zoning board, or the tennis club. We *do* together rather than *be* together—it's a style of relating more common among men than among women, for whom "being" is an essential ingredient of most if not all our relationships.

If we worry about being overwhelmed by involvement with others, we probably have thick interpersonal boundaries that limit our participation in inappropriate relationships; we're careful and organized in our dealings with people and aware of the expectations of our group, class, or society, but we also have a capacity for getting along and living with others peacefully. And when we do connect on a deeper emotional level with someone, it doesn't naturally follow that our overall boundaries become thinner or more permeable; instead, we place another thick boundary around the relationship to protect it from those outside it.

Hannah's boundaries are much thicker than Caitlin's, yet the two have a "soul-to-soul" connection that's surprising between two such different women. "I'm always surprised when people say that she's so distant and aloof; that's not my experience of her at all," comments Caitlin. "Maybe I just came along at a point where she needed to open up to someone, and it happened to be me. But she still doesn't let anyone else get too close." Thinner or more permeable boundaries make us more inclined to get involved in relationships quickly, without the same concern for the approval of others or the preplanning that people with thicker boundaries often evidence. If our boundaries are thin, we tend to be guided by immediate feelings of closeness or trust and follow our feelings and impulses in the way we enter as well as leave relationships. That explains why Melinda eloped with a man she'd known for a month and why Karen won't ask a potential lover to take an HIV test before they have unprotected sex. It explains why Lisa hired a nanny without checking her references and why Pat ends an affair as soon as it's run its course, if not before, explaining that what she likes best is the falling in love part, but she's not real big on what comes after that: "There's nothing I'd rather not do than 'work' on a relationship," she says. "Call me a traitor to my sex, but I'm not interested. If you have to work on it all the time, when do you get to just enjoy it?"

Both love and friendship satisfy some of the same core needs; to be able to count on the other, to feel happy in their company, to feel mutually understood, recognized, and appreciated. But intimacy requires greater exclusivity, passion, and commitment than friendship; it's also often based on an idealization of the other—a willing suspension of disbelief and delusion, as Kyra puts it. "I love my husband in spite of his flaws," she says, "but I love my close friends because of them."

Interpersonal boundaries define mutual understandings in relationships, guide behavior, and establish rules for interaction. But the very establishment of boundaries increases the likelihood that conflicts will occur because those boundaries, in all probability, will be violated on occasion. Emotional trespass is more frequent and likely among friends and acquaintances than it is with strangers, whose intrusions rarely touch our deepest feelings, or with intimates, where boundaries tend to be thinner, more relaxed, and less clearly delineated. "Betrayal is the terrorism of friendship," says Letty Pogrebin, a feminist writer. "You can't prepare for it because you never know when it will strike, or worry about it because it would poison your life, but once you're its victim, it's like a slice off your soul."

The Boundaries of Gender

Our sense of self is bound up in our women friends in an intensity and depth that's not present in our relationships with (most) men. With women friends we tend to repeat or react to old conflicts with our mothers, or compensate for them by being better friends to one another than our mothers were to us. The same reworking of past problems with our sisters or other close female relatives happens in many women's friendships. Natalie's sister's manic depression made their relationship problematic during most of their adolescence. In her often turbulent twenty-year friendship with Lynn, who's also bipolar, she's able to be the consistently loving, understanding "sister" she wasn't able to be with her own. In fact, in almost all her connections with women, Natalie makes more compromises and accommodations, is more tolerant and understanding than they are, because of the guilt she still feels about her anger, jealousy, and exasperation with her sister. Reba's friendships with women who are older or in other ways senior to her are colored by her difficult childhood; every one of these relationships becomes a search for the perfect mother she never had and ends with Reba turning into the demanding, narcissistic one she always disappointed.

For many women, the line between true friendship and casual acquaintanceship is a very fine one, blurred by the expectation of some kind of emotional exchange. That makes it harder for us than it is for men to accept the limited or utilitarian nature of some nonintimate relationships without feeling that we're cheating or being cheated, using or being used. This is partly traceable to the different developmental imperatives of gender; while men's psychological tasks are separation and individuation, women's are relational and affiliative. As the psychologist Jean Baker Miller points out, for many women the threat of disruption of an affiliation is perceived not just as a loss of relationship but as something closer to a total loss of self. But much goes on between people, men and women alike—that's what interpersonal means. "Friend" is only one definition, which is why the dimensions of boundaries themselves—permeability, flexibility, and complexity—determine where on the continuum between separate and connected we meet.

Your boundary style determines what you bring to or take from your social world. In the next chapter, you'll see how to use the tools of boundary intelligence to get the comfort of closeness as well as the clarity of distance in those relationships, which are a vital part of your life: as Ingrid says, "Sex may be the carbohydrates in my life, but friendship is the protein."

CHAPTER 9

Who Can You Call at Three in the Morning?

I get to Starbucks a few minutes early and settle down with a double latte and the crossword puzzle. On the dot of the hour Marissa arrives at the crowded, bustling café. "Do you mind if we move?" she asks. "There's more room at that table by the window."

I suck in my stomach, trying not to spill hot coffee on my neighbor's lap as I squeeze through the narrow space between the tables. It's a cold, damp day and there's always a draft near the window, but I comply because Marissa has a "thing" about sitting close to other people.

If Marissa and I were animals, I'd be a Labrador retriever and she'd be a Persian cat. I'd be wagging my tail and licking people's faces and finding someone to scratch behind my ears, while she prowled elegantly around the room, carefully observing the inhabitants before choosing one to favor with her company. And even then, she'd keep her distance.

Marissa and I go way back, but despite our twenty-year friendship she still prefaces a confidence with, "Please don't tell anyone about this," even though I never have. She still gets that opaque look in her eyes, as if she can't remember where we met, whenever I get too close to something she's touchy or sensitive about, and sometimes when I make the mistake of starting a sentence with, "If you want my advice," she stops me with a firm, unquestionable, "No, I don't" before I can get another word in.

Marissa and I have some of the big things in common, like how we were raised, where we went to college, how we make our living, and what we think is funny. We share a passion for antique jewelry, trashy novels, and any movie that's not billed as "a triumph of the human spirit." But the biggest difference between us—the one that nearly nipped a promising friendship in the bud before it had a chance to bloom and still threatens it on occasion—is where each of us draws the line. Not just the line between us, or even between us and other people, but between what's private and what's public, what's acceptable and what isn't, what's safe and what's scary, what and whom we embrace, and what and whom we keep at a distance.

In a word, Marissa and I have a lot of what she was the first to characterize as boundary issues, and I used to call her *mishegas*, which is a Yiddish word for someone else's neuroses. Marissa's interpersonal boundaries are as different from mine as, well, a cat's from a dog's. Hers are fixed, protected, relatively impermeable, and very well defined, while mine are more like my waistline—there somewhere, but looser, more flexible, and harder to find unless you bump into them by accident.

Marissa and I manage to keep our friendship vital and important to us both despite (and sometimes because of) our very different boundary styles, even though it's not always easy. We have clearer, more explicit boundaries with each other than most friends usually have, so we avoid as many instances of emotional trespass as we can see coming, and when it happens, despite our best efforts, we deal with it immediately instead of letting it fester. We negotiate boundary crossings like porcupines—very carefully—and understand that sometimes staying inside our own lines is better for our friendship than trying for common ground, especially when it comes to some basic differences in our values.

Because I know that the boundaries around my relationship

with Marissa are more dyadic than they are in many of my friend-ships that tend to overlap, I don't just assume that it would be okay with her if I invited someone else to join us on an antiquing expedition, and I can tell her about a party I had without fearing she'd be hurt if I didn't invite her; in fact, usually she's pleased that she doesn't have to make up an excuse for not coming. There are some questions I'd never ask her, some comments I'd make casually to another friend but rarely to her. And while it may seem like I'm the one who's doing all the work here, she accommodates my boundary style, too, by being more flexible in the permeability of her boundaries than she is with most people and more proactive than I sometimes am in finding ways we can be close as well as separate.

Friends or Lovers—Must We Be One or the Other?

Generally, the way people interact with others depends on a certain fit, and the most important considerations in fit have to do with two things: the specific interaction—its context, content, and meaning—and each person's boundary style. But boundary misfit doesn't have to be the death knell in a relationship, as long as you recognize that it exists. When you focus your awareness on the boundaries that connect and separate you from someone, it can guide your expecta-tions of the particular relationship as well as your behavior in it. Often this will mean making some adjustment in your own bound-ary style—for instance, being more flexible to improve the fit, or using your complexity to tune in some "channels" more clearly and tune out the static on others. It's boundary complexity that makes it possible to develop a good, albeit platonic and nonromantic friend-ship with a man who's "just not that into you," as the current cliché has it; just because he doesn't want to sleep with you (or vice versa) doesn't mean there aren't other possibilities in the friendship. But unless you can accept the fact that his pheromones aren't set off by yours, and avoid trying to turn a willing friend into a reluctant lover, these possibilities will probably never materialize.

Men often feel excluded from and/or envious of the depths of women's friendships. Says Marcus, "My friendships with men aren't very complex—they're good companions for some things, competitors for many—especially jobs and women—and scorecards for your own successes and failures. On the whole, I prefer women. They make the best friends—that is, once the sexual thing is settled." He added, "Gay men have better relationships with straight women than I do."

Many women feel that their friendships with gay men are generally less stressful and richer in some kinds of mutuality than their heterosexual involvements. "The sexual thing is usually settled at the outset, so maybe there's more energy available for other kinds of sharing," says Roberta, a set designer with many close, important gay male friends. "Of course, sometimes, especially when I'm with several of them at the same time, I feel irrelevant and even invisible. One time an actor I really love—a gay guy—introduced me to a fellow who happened to be very attractive. I thought he was straight, and when my friend told me he wasn't, I said, 'What a waste,' not realizing my gaffe until he said—through gritted teeth—'For whom?'"

There are women who refuse to go out with gay men; it's humiliating, says one, and another calls it pointless. You can't argue with comments like that; as Roberta says: "I know some people who still think Nixon was framed, and as long as we don't talk politics, we manage quite well." And there are women whose only close male friends are gay, a result of deep hurts inflicted in previous romantic relationships; you can't argue with them, either. There are still others, like Emma, who try to rehabilitate gay men, which is how they characterize their efforts to set them straight; there's not that much distance, except stylistically, between her and that stereotypical redneck who thinks that all a lesbian needs to convince her of the error of her sexual preference is a night of love with him. Says Madelyn, who teaches women's studies, "In a culture that still connects suppression of feelings with masculine identity, only gay men have the freedom to acknowledge what, and that, they feel. Gay men understand the language of emotions because they've been hard-pressed to suppress or ignore the frequent pain of living gay in a mainly straight world. Having discarded some culturally cued male behavior, they're freer to ignore some of its less appealing aspects and tolerate playfulness, spontaneity, even theatricality. Most straight men are embarrassed by such behavior—they call it feminine, childish, and silly."

It's not "the sexual thing" that makes close friendship without romance difficult—it's the emotional thing.

What I Like about You Is How Much You're (Not) Like Me

What makes a relationship between two friends with no romantic agenda successful—or even possible—is understanding and respecting how and where his or her boundary style—especially interpersonal boundary style—is different from yours. And while the interpersonal section of the Boundary Style Questionnaire is a wide-angle snapshot of your boundaries in the social surround as well as the relative distance you keep (or don't) from people in general, it doesn't measure closeness or intimacy in specific relationships like those you have with your inner circle—those A-list friends who are significant contributors to your sense of self. Considering each of your three closest friends separately, complete this quiz on the nature of your friendship boundaries.

Friendly Boundaries Quiz

Read each answer carefully, as they can vary, before responding.

1. I'm more tactful and considerate with her than candid and direct. _____
   1 = never   2 = sometimes   3 = often   4 = always

2. Conflict with her makes me anxious. _____
   1 = never   2 = sometimes   3 = often   4 = always

3. What she thinks about me affects how I feel about myself. _____
   1 = never   2 = sometimes   3 = often   4 = always

4. There are certain confidences I don't trust her with. _____
   1 = never   2 = sometimes   3 = often   4 = always

5. I say what I think to her, regardless of how it might affect our friendship. _____
   1 = never   2 = sometimes   3 = often   4 = always

6. She thinks she knows me, but she really doesn't. _____
   1 = always true   2 = often true   3 = sometimes true
   4 = not true

7. I'm the one who compromises when we disagree. _____
   1 = never   2 = sometimes   3 = often   4 = always

8. When she's unhappy, it's gets me down, too. _____
   1 = never   2 = sometimes   3 = often   4 = always

9. Whatever she did or said, it couldn't destroy our friendship. _____
   1 = not true   2 = sometimes true   3 = often true
   4 = always true

10. Our friendship matters as much to her as it does to me. _____
    1 = not true   2 = sometimes true   3 = often true
    4 = always true

Total _____

Some of these items may seem very similar to the intimate boundaries section of the Boundary Style Questionnaire; that's because, absent the erotic nature of those relationships, women's friendships are often more intimate than those with their husbands or lovers. Here's proof: when you compare your score on this questionnaire as it relates to the person you consider your closest friend with your intimate boundaries score that references your relationship with your lover or spouse, the numbers will likely be within a point or two of each other. Since a key aspect of intimacy is self-disclosure, women tend to self-disclose more with women friends than they do with their male partners. Says Beatrice, "At least they listen and care." Also, in most cases those revelations don't threaten the relationship: "I can tell Tess that sometimes I hate my life and wonder why I ever got married, but it doesn't change my marriage . . . it may even help it by letting me blow off steam safely," says Ruth. And because women are more relationally adept than most men—it's in our DNA—we're usually more skilled at mutuality and empathy, too. At least, that's the general consensus. But not every good, solid friendship is an intimate one; many are more mutual than others, and some can surmount the absence of empathy if they offer other rewards.

You Can't Always Get What You Want

Corinne and Meg have been friends since graduate school. Although they live at opposite ends of the country, they both travel frequently. When Corinne's in New York, it's a given that she'll stay at Meg's apartment, and when Meg's in L.A., at least twice a year, she does the same. They e-mail back and forth a few times a week, and every month or so they have a lengthy phone conversation in which they bring each other up to date on all the events in their lives. Much of it is related to their careers—"I know the names of all the important people in Meg's professional life and lots of details about them. I'm pretty conversant with the politics in her office and her projects and deadlines," says Corinne. She also knows a great deal about Meg's other friends (including those she hasn't met but hears about), the state of her health, and her problems with her siblings. "That's the kind of stuff we talk about, along with books, politics, fashion, and shopping—we can spend an hour on the phone without running out of things to share," Corinne adds. "When there's a man in either of our lives, we talk about that, too—it's like a date's not over until we've discussed and dissected it!"

Yet in spite of their common interests and all the time they invest in their relationship, Corinne and Meg aren't particularly intimate friends, because their inner lives are rarely open to each other. "Meg just doesn't open up that way—not to me, and not to anyone as far as I know," says Corinne. "When I talk about my feelings, what I think of as the core of who I am, she listens, but I don't think she hears or even understands. And sometimes she can be very insensitive." It took Corinne a long time to get over what she considered a betrayal of the boundaries of their friendship. "On my fortieth birthday I invited my six closest friends to celebrate with me at a spa for the weekend . . . I'd just gotten a financial windfall and I was picking up the tab. I just assumed Meg was coming, but when I double-checked because I had to finalize the reservations, she told me she wasn't. That was it . . . no explanation, no excuse, no nothing. To this day, she's never referred to that invitation or talked about why she didn't come. I ended up realizing that in spite of what I think we both consider an important friendship, it's missing a key ingredient, at least for me . . . she just has hardly any interest in my deepest feelings and none in sharing hers."

Corinne tried reaching across the gap between them. "I e-mailed her a few days after the party and told her how much I'd missed her. I asked if there was anything wrong between us and said I was concerned about our relationship. But she just didn't respond to any of that, although she did to other stuff I wrote about in the same message. It was like my feelings about her ignoring the event went into a void somewhere. But nothing else has changed in how we interact with each other. We still talk regularly, tell each other our stories and news, see each other whenever we can. I've just accepted that she and I have very different emotional lives, and she's not interested in mine or even her own, for that matter. So I don't look for that kind of closeness with her—I just enjoy what we do share and get what I need in the way of empathy and understanding in my other friendships."

Many women wouldn't be able to get over this kind of slight in a close friendship, but given Corinne's high scores in boundary complexity, it's understandable; she's able to take what Meg has to offer without worrying about what she won't or can't share or provide, and focus instead on the many important things they have in common, while looking to other friends for emotional sharing. (Interestingly enough, Meg also scored high in boundary complexity, although in flexibility and all areas of boundary permeability she scored in the low to medium range.)

By contrast, Lily and Lois open up their hearts and feelings to each other—both are process oriented, and they do a lot of talking about the quality of their friendship. Yet sometimes even Lois gets tired of analyzing their psyches and their relationship: "Sometimes I want to talk about other things, like books or movies or money, but the conversation always ends up being about whether I'm too judgmental—which I am!—or she's too 'woo woo'—which she is," says Lois. "To her, intimacy is only about feelings . . . and frankly, sometimes this girl just wants to have fun!" Lily's scores on boundary permeability are significantly higher than Lois's, especially her inner and intimate boundaries, but her flexibility scores are much lower—she's not as capable as Lois is of adjusting her boundary permeability. By the numbers, their overall boundary styles seem similar, since Lois's complexity scores were greater than Lily's. But the differences are telling; Lois is able to connect more easily on more levels with more people than Lily, for whom a relationship without a great deal of sharing and processing of feelings is a waste of time and emotional energy.

Do They Feel the Same Way about You—and Does It Matter?

Here's another way to look at your friendships. Take the quiz on page 166, the one you filled out for three of your closest friends, as if you were those women (or men, if there are some with whom you have close, nonromantic friendships). Given what you know about them, consider how they'd answer the questions in terms of their relationship with you. Compare your responses with what you think theirs would be; it's another way of looking at how mutual your connections with them are and how meaningful or important you think you are to each other. You might even want to ask them to fill out the questionnaire, too, but don't make it seem like a test of your friendship, and make certain you reassure them that they don't have to share their individual answers or their total score with you if they don't want to—respect their boundaries!

One benefit of this exercise is that it clarifies whether you're getting what you want in your friendships—the right balance of autonomy and intimacy—and whether your boundary style is complex enough to accommodate friendships that may be lacking in closeness in some areas but have openings in others. Because good friendships based on common interests, proximity, and social exchange can fill some of the empty places in your life, increase the breadth of your personal and professional reach, and be fulfilling in their own right. Like Corinne, you may realize that emotional intimacy—or the lack of it—doesn't have to be a deal-breaker in every friendship, and like Lois, you may need some less intense or process-oriented relationships to meet some of your other social needs. Different boundary styles may make it harder to resonate to a shared emotional bandwidth, but plenty of perfectly good friendships have been built on other foundations.

Competing Loyalties and Inadvertent Betrayals

Unlike kinship and marriage, friendship is a relationship with no formal boundaries and implicit rather than explicit expectations and assumptions. As such, it's rife with opportunities for accidental trespass, inadvertent betrayals, misunderstandings, and the stresses caused by competing loyalties.

Loyalty and betrayal have long been viewed as personality traits or characterological tendencies. But in the context of relationships rather than individual traits, both are social experiences in which we're called upon to balance the needs of self and other(s) in a crosscurrent of competing and oppositional loyalty demands . . . as any woman knows who's ever been tempted to take up with a friend's former boyfriend, break a date with a chum because a man (or even another woman) called with a better offer, break off a friendship with someone who fell out with another friend, take sides in a personal dispute between two people on her A-list, or faced a dilemma between the friendship and some other demand. It might be a demand that stresses your own limits, like the tug of war you feel when a friend just needs you to listen to her vent and you've got a deadline to meet at the office or a family waiting for dinner. It might also be a matter of competing internal loyalties or expectations: "Bella and I have been friends for a long time, and we've always supported each other's decisions and choices even if we didn't necessarily think they were the right ones," said Cass. "But when she had an abortion, I felt an enormous conflict between our friendship and my own values, which are strongly prolife. I wish she hadn't told me, especially since she's always known that about me. On the other hand, one thing we've always been is totally honest with each other. So I have two conflicts going on here—between what I expect in the friendship and between my values and that friendship. One thing I know is that things are never going to be the same between us again."

Cass's boundary complexity is in the low range, and because she is so enmeshed in her relationships—she is them, she doesn't just have them—she can't separate Bella's choice from the one she would have made or reach across the bridge between them and focus on those values they share.

Sometimes it's necessary to make your boundaries explicit rather than assume a friend understands where they are; while it's always better to do that in advance of a situation, usually it's only after the lines have been crossed that you think you should have. Knowing how Cass felt about abortion, Bella might have chosen not to tell her that she was pregnant or what she did about it; knowing her friend was somewhat casual about birth control, Cass might have said, "If you got pregnant and decided to have an abortion, I'd have a really hard time accepting that, in spite of how much I care about you."

On a lighter note, if you really don't want a friend to take up with an old boyfriend—or even a guy you've got your eye on—put it on the table between you. Don't pretend it won't rankle when you know it will and expect that a good sportsmanship medal will soothe your hurt feelings. "I thought we were done with this sort of stuff in high school," Amanda said when Harriet went into a tizzy of "How could you's" after Amanda accepted a date with a man they'd both met at the same party. "She was very excited about him—when he took her phone number, she was sure he'd call. But a few days later he phoned me—I'd told him where I worked—and asked me to lunch. What was I going to say, that I couldn't accept because my friend liked him, too?" No, but when they were dishing the party she might have told Harriet that she was also intrigued by the guy they'd both been eyeing and that she considered him fair game. If at the same time she'd done something to solidify her bond with Harriet—make plans with her to do something the following weekend, for example—it might have reconfirmed her loyalty to their friendship.

The Enemy of My Friend Is My Enemy

Sometimes women's relationships with other women (not to mention men!) *do* seem reminiscent of high school, where the price of one particular friendship was sometimes the cost of another and a falling-out between two people forced the realignment of all their other friendships. Coalitions, alliances, and other examples of triangulation are the substance of peer relations in adolescence as well as in the family, which is why the more differentiated and less enmeshed your family boundaries were, the more capable you may be of making and keeping your friendships more separate from than connected to one another and regulating distance and closeness as you choose to in each one. As an adult, though, you have other ways to define yourself besides who your friends are and more options with those you have now than you might have had back then. You're also (probably) more skilled at balancing competing demands, understanding when loyalty to yourself, your beliefs, and your values takes precedence over loyalty to another person, and accepting that every slight (or what you consider one) can be an opportunity to clarify your boundaries and connect across them rather than an intentional trespass or a betrayal of the relationship. You may be extremely sensitive and open to your psychological surround, but the more you can regulate that permeability—the more flexible you can be in closing down when it's necessary to protect yourself emotionally and opening up when it seems safe to do so—the more satisfied you'll be in all your friendships.

Why Women Make Such a Big Deal Out of Friendship and (Most) Men Don't

Much has been studied and written about the psychological importance of friendship in the female experience. One of the hallmarks of female development is lifelong intimacy with women friends. Although our capacity for intimacy and mutual support is highly developed in comparison with men, friendship between women is too often an exchange of selflessness instead of mutual growth. We tend to take excessive responsibility for our friends' needs and feelings, and fears of envy, success, and conflict often plague our relationships with them. As a result, in the name of friendship we may neglect our own boundaries, ignore theirs, and make regulating distance and closeness a global opening up or shutting down of those boundaries rather than an incremental adjustment to them; both setting and stretching boundaries causes conflict, fear, and/or tension for many women. Yet real friendship flourishes when we discover that expressing our personal needs for more or less intimacy in the relationship enhances the connection rather than threatens it. We need people in our life who can resonate to our feelings or bear them with us; when we can't respond to a friend this way and withdraw, disconnect, or disengage, it feels to the other like a boundary violation and even a punishment for daring to be vulnerable. But when we know we're not up to that task and can communicate that honestly as a message about ourselves rather than one about them, and use our boundary complexity to reach across the divide and connect on another dimension of the relationship, we can not only preserve but also strengthen it.

Friends are participants not just in our lives but in our personal psychological development, too. We gain competence and initiative in the context of important relationships; we discover ourselves when we are listened to with a caring understanding, as the psychologist Carl Rogers says. But we also tend to idealize our friends in ways that men do not; while trust, honesty, respect, commitment, safety, support, generosity, loyalty, constancy, mutuality, understanding, and acceptance are the qualities we deem desirable and even essential in a friend, as Dr. Lillian Rubin writes, "it's often this wish list we're referring to, rather than the realities of the relationship." It's when the fantasy meets the reality and the differences in boundary styles aren't minimized or ignored but understood and accepted that friendship grows out of the high school stage and into its necessary and enriching place in our relational lives.

Sharing your inner life, feeling close to others, and trusting them with your feelings aren't always key elements in every friendship. But some of each has to be present in order to sustain more than the most casual connection. Social intimacy isn't the same thing as person-to-person intimacy—it's more related to characterological traits like introversion and extraversion and more closely allied with interpersonal boundaries that define your connection to the general social surround than with specific others. Here's a quiz that focuses on this aspect of your interpersonal boundaries.

Social Intimacy Quiz

Please read each answer key before responding as some answers are different or reverse-scored.

1. When I have leisure time, I choose to spend it
    with other people.   _____
    1 = never   2 = sometimes   3 = often   4 = always

2. I keep most personal information to myself or
    only share it with my closest friends.   _____
    1 = never   2 = sometimes   3 = often   4 = always

3. I'm demonstrative and affectionate with most
    people.   _____
    1 = never   2 = sometimes   3 = often   4 = always

4. I try to encourage or support people when
   they're unhappy.   _____
   1 = never true   2 = sometimes true   3 = often true
   4 = always true

5. I have nonromantic relationships with men that
   are important to me.   _____
   1 = never   2 = sometimes   3 = often   4 = always

6. It's hard for me to understand or empathize with
   others' feelings if they're very different from
   my own.   _____
   1 = always true   2 = often true   3 = sometimes true
   4 = never true

7. When I'm depressed, I need other people to cheer
   me up.   _____
   1 = never   2 = sometimes   3 = often   4 = always

8. If others don't notice or pay attention to me,
   I feel invisible.   _____
   1 = never   2 = sometimes   3 = often   4 = always

9. I'm very interested in what's happening to
   people I know.   _____
   1 = never   2 = sometimes   3 = often   4 = always

10. I don't know my neighbors and prefer it that way.   _____
    1 = always true   2 = often true   3 = sometimes true
    4 = never true

Total   _____

On Putting All Your Eggs in
One Basket

Not every woman is "multisocial," as Petra describes herself; she's
at the center of several different formal and informal networks of
people, which is partly due to her naturally gregarious and outgoing

personality, but even more to the position she found herself in after she was divorced. "I'd been isolated in a bad marriage for a long time, and as a result, I had very few friends when it ended . . . none, really, since I was ashamed that I'd stayed in an abusive situation for so long and embarrassed about people knowing it." She was also a single mother, too concerned about economic survival and too tired from coping with the demands of a job and two small kids to put any effort into making new friends. "There were women in my abuse support group, but I really didn't want to see them outside of it—we didn't have much in common, or at least, I didn't want to think we might," she said. But shortly after her divorce, when the kids were with their father and she "really let myself feel the loneliness," she had what she describes as a "Scarlett at Tara experience . . . I pounded my pillow and cried, 'I'll never be lonely again!'"

In the six years since that time, Petra rebuilt her relational life one friend at a time. "I took them where I found them—at work, the gym, the PTA, even someone I met in the dentist's waiting room who was reading a book I'd loved—we had lunch together a few days later and she invited me to join her book club." She hasn't shared the nitty-gritty of her former life with many of those people—"I have the one-, two-, and three-sentence versions, and I've really only opened up about it to one woman," she reports. Instead, she's found or made common ground with people of different ages and backgrounds. One of her most rewarding new friendships is with a woman thirty years her senior whose perspective on life, says Petra, has widened her own, "along with her no-excuses and no-bullshit attitude, which has really rubbed off on me." Petra works hard at these relationships; she remembers birthdays and special occasions, checks in with her friends on a regular basis, and goes the extra distance when compromise is called for. "But I'm pretty careful about not being taken advantage of," she adds. "There's this warning bell that goes off inside me when somebody tries to do that that makes me stop and think, what's going on here? And if it's what it feels like, rather than a flashback to what used to happen when I was married, I stop it right there. You know, lots of people don't realize when they're crossing your lines . . . once you tell them, it clears the air." Which is a pretty good description of not only learning from experience but exercising boundary intelligence.

Other women don't seem to need a wide circle of friends. Trina counts on Val for companionship, emotional sharing, and validation, but when Val fell in love, their friendship changed, which usually happens. "I kind of expected it," Trina says, "because I've been there myself. But still, it really hurt. I had no one to talk to, share with, or even go to a movie with . . . at least, no one who really knew me, that I could be myself with." Since then, Trina has made a few new friends, but primarily with women who are already married or in intimate relationships. "At least then you know where you stand, you know that's going to take precedence most of the time, so you're not disappointed. I have a few more people in my life than I did when Val and I were so close, but something's missing— I don't really feel like I'm getting as much intimacy as I would like, so I think I've tended to retreat in some ways even as I'm reaching out in others."

Everyone's needs for social intimacy are different; for one person, a single good friend is more important than a host of others. Generally the more permeable your boundaries are, the greater your desire for multiple friendships, but unless your boundary flexibility is as high as your permeability, you may find it hard to sustain relationships with those whose boundary style is very different from yours; your openness will feel threatening to them and you may feel short-changed in the reciprocity department. But using boundary intelligence to adjust your permeability when the friendship requires it and managing your complexity so you can accept what another person has to offer—even though you might want more or different things from the relationship—makes it more likely that it can grow into something closer to your heart's desire. Because the more complex your boundaries are, the more aware you will be in every relationship of the difference between community, which is feeling connected to other people, and attachment, which is necessary for the development of a truly mutual friendship.

CHAPTER 10

In and Out of Bounds
at the Office

All boundary crossings are precarious—it's the porcupine effect again—and no boundaries offer more possibilities for misfit, trespass, and confusion than the one between home and office—even if the "office" is a home-based business or a desk in the corner of the den—or between you and your organization.

How satisfied you are with the work you do, the culture of the industry or the organization you do it in, and the degree to which it dominates (or doesn't) the rest of your life have as much to do with your boundary style as your relationships with colleagues, managers, employees, clients, and others with whom you interact in the professional arena. As Ernest Hartmann pointed out, people with thin inner boundaries tend to work in atypical, creative, or artistic fields, while those in blue- or white-collar jobs tend to have thicker, less permeable ones. And flexibility and complexity also influence the separation or connection between the personal and professional aspects of your identity. So when we talk about the boundaries of career, we're talking about two different types of boundaries; the work/life boundary as well as the one that structures your work environment and determines your performance and satisfaction in it.

When What You Do Is Who You Are—
and When It Isn't

Some people gravitate toward a blended life—Rachel calls hers "seamless"—where the two dominant aspects of identity are hard to distinguish. Like many writers, what Rachel does is inextricably aligned with who she is. She admits that this merger of the personal and the professional has its disadvantages. "When my relationships, activities, or other commitments aren't going well, my work is affected—it practically grinds to a halt. Every phrase or sentence I manage to turn out feels like its been extruded from a very constricted place. And when my work isn't on track, I find it hard to concentrate on anything else or get much satisfaction from other areas of my life. When either my work or my life is going poorly, the other suffers. I'm not fully present in either place—I have trouble keeping my emotions and ruminations from distracting me."

Rachel's boundary style reflects that—her inner boundaries are much more permeable than either her intimate or her interpersonal ones. "I live in my head a lot of the time," she says. "Both my feelings and my imagination. My thoughts and emotions and sensations kind of blend together. And sometimes I don't even notice other people unless they're right in my face, even my family. I can't tell you how many times my kids say, 'Earth to Mom, come in.'"

Interestingly, when things are going well in one aspect of Rachel's life, it seems to ratchet up the other to a better level of functioning—when the words are flowing, so is everything else. "I have more energy, more enthusiasm, more competence and confidence and joy, and it shows in everything from my health to my relationship with my husband and kids. It's the time before that, before I actually sit down to write, when I'm working out an idea or an image sticks in my mind and I can't figure out what to do with it or what it means . . . that's when my work/life boundaries are hard to manage."

Second-Shifting in Work, Life, and Love

But what Rachel doesn't have more of when everything's going smoothly and she's on a roll is time, which for many women is the devil in the detail of balancing the demands of the personal and the professional. Those who work in more structured environments than hers might seem to have a built-in boundary between life and work, one that's less permeable and flexible than that of a writer, an artist, or a musician, or even an entrepreneur or a freelancer like Riva, a publicist, or Cynthia, a boutique owner, both of whom say they're never not thinking about work, even when they're not doing it. "Being in business for yourself is like always having homework," says Riva.

Even the gifted cartoonist Nicole Hollander, who created such memorable characters as The Woman Who Does Everything More Beautifully Than You and The Woman Who Lies in Her Personal Journal, can't conceive of The Woman Who Has Time for Everything. That's not surprising, given how much of the "work" of life women do, from cleaning, cooking, and child care—what the writer Sylvia Hewitt calls "second-shifting"—to much of the emotional management of relationships with their partners, family, and friends. For most women the work/life boundary remains more permeable and fluid than it does for men, even when their professional environment is enclosed by time clocks (real or metaphorical), rules, roles, and a structure that distinguishes it from the personal sphere.

But that doesn't mean that even if you work in a nine-to-five job, keeping the lines between life and work clear is an easy task. You may turn off your computer, clear off your desk, and close your door when you leave the office, firm, or bank, but even while you're fixing dinner or reading your child a bedtime story you may also be mentally rehearsing the presentation you're making to the marketing team the next day or wondering how the audit's going. While you're sharing a romantic moment with your partner or coaching the soccer team, another part of your brain may be roughing out the brief that's due by the end of the week or thinking about your performance review.

That's multitasking, which is jargon for doing a lot of things at once; it's also a synonym for letting your work spill over into your life, and vice versa. Research into how the often-conflicting tugs of the personal and the professional affect both domains indicates that spillover from work contributes more to the prediction of family stress than spillover from family does for work. Emotional exhaustion plays a central role in the work domains, while in the family, personal accomplishment at work is the most central component of spillover stress, as measured by burnout, mood, work overload, work-family interference, support, and marital satisfaction. Another study supports the conclusion that while work and family boundaries are asymmetrically permeable, family boundaries are more permeable than work boundaries—work interferes with family life more frequently than family life interferes with work. But in this study of 278 men and 353 women, there was no evidence of gender differences in the pattern of asymmetry; in other words, the dynamics of work and family boundaries operate similarly among men and women.

How permeable is your work/life boundary? As in the other quizzes in this book, the higher the score, the more permeable the boundary, but the score may also indicate why you're satisfied (or not) with your work, the environment you do it in, and the meaning you make of it.

Work/Life Boundary Quiz

Please read each answer key before responding as some answers are different or reverse-scored.

1. My personal and professional friendships
   often overlap.   ———
   1 = never   2 = sometimes   3 = often   4 = always

2. When I leave work, I don't think about it; when I'm off duty, I'm really off.   _____

   1 = always   2 = often   3 = sometimes   4 = never

3. It's important to feel personally closer to the people I work with.   _____

   1 = never true   2 = sometimes true   3 = often true
   4 = always true

4. My performance review affects how I feel about myself.   _____

   1 = never true   2 = sometimes true   3 = often true
   4 = always true

5. When I have problems at home, it's hard to focus on work.   _____

   1 = never   2 = sometimes   3 = often   4 = always

6. I'm open about my personal life with my colleagues.   _____

   1 = never   2 = sometimes   3 = often   4 = always

7. I'd rather work with other people than by myself.   _____

   1 = never true   2 = sometimes true   3 = often true
   4 = always true

8. When people are having personal difficulties, their colleagues and managers should cut them some slack and make allowances for their performance.   _____

   1 = never true   2 = sometimes true   3 = often true
   4 = always true

9. My family's needs take precedence over my work commitments.   _____

   1 = never   2 = sometimes   3 = often   4 = always

10. Where someone is in the company hierarchy
     doesn't affect my friendship with him or her.   _____
     1 = never true   2 = sometimes true   3 = often true
     4 = always true

Total   _____

The higher your score on this quiz, the more permeable and
fluid the boundary is apt to be between your personal life and your
professional agenda. If the work you do, the conditions you do it
under, and those you do it with or for don't provide enough opportunities for achieving at least some of your goals in both domains,
you're at risk for burnout, stress, and emotional as well as logistical
overload. But if your boundary flexibility is high enough, you may
be able to tune out distractions that diminish your effectiveness at
work and clutter your personal life with a briefcase that's never
empty.

Blended Relationships and Other
Boundary Crossings

When Toni moved to Manhattan and joined an advertising agency
as an account manager, Maureen, a copywriter, was a one-woman
welcome wagon. She helped Toni find an apartment, a dentist, and
a health club; showed her where to buy designer clothes at half
price; and invited her to join her reading group. But Toni grew
uncomfortable with Maureen's constant demands for attention at
the office as well as after hours and tried "dialing back the friendship," as she puts it. "I begged off the Friday nights at the movies,
the Saturdays at the flea market, until she finally took the hint,
but what happened after that was like a B movie," Toni shudders.
"She told the partners lies about me—that I was sleeping with a

client and interviewing with competitors. She effectively ruined my chances for getting anywhere at the agency." At her next job, Toni avoided getting close to any colleagues. "I really changed my way of dealing with people. I said nothing about my personal life, avoided all office functions, and never even had lunch with a coworker. I just kept my head down and did my work." But at the end of her six-month probationary period, Toni's manager said, "We're a people organization—we think of ourselves as a family. But you don't seem to be comfortable here . . . maybe you'd be happier somewhere else."

Like Toni, Liza discovered that blurring the lines between friendship and business can be tricky. She was promoted to a supervisory position over Jan, who'd been a bridesmaid at her wedding. When Jan failed to meet an important deadline for the third time in a row, Liza had to fire her. "How could she do such a thing? She knew I was having problems at home with my kid," Jan sniffed. "A real friend wouldn't have done that." But Liza felt she had no choice. "I offered her an assistant, I extended her deadlines as long as I could, and I did a lot of her work myself. I even suggested she take a leave until she could get her problems with her daughter solved and get her own act together. She kept telling me she was fine, she'd get the work done, no problem. But ultimately it was my job at stake—and my best friend was compromising my professionalism."

Linda, who started at an insurance company as a customer service representative, leapfrogged over colleagues in a series of promotions. As she rose through the ranks, her former office mates didn't invite her out as often, and she became more guarded about what she discussed with them. She remained close with a former colleague, Daniele, who had hired her as an intern when Linda was in college; less than ten years later, Linda was Daniele's supervisor, and while the two refrained from talking at work about the family vacations they took together, it was no secret that they were close friends. It was harder for Daniele than it was for Linda; people sought confidential information about Linda as well as her views and opinions from Daniele and often used her as a sounding board to thrash out issues or proposals on which they needed Linda's approval. But the women's close relationship also enabled Daniele to take liberties with her boss that other subordinates would be unlikely to try. And Linda, who's now the company's president, admits, "The hardest thing is acting like a boss in front of friends."

Improperly managing boundary issues like the transition from friend to supervisor is one reason why many women's otherwise promising careers falter. "Because there are so many women in the workplace now, we tend to think boundaries are a lot looser today. But in fact, they're not—they're tighter and more important than ever," according to Barbara Reinhold, the director of the Smith College Development Office and the author of *Toxic Work*. In big cities where newcomers use the office as a social nexus, and among singles without families or extensive commitments outside their jobs, the work/life boundary is often blurred; friendships and romances may flourish in these circumstances, but because of them, some careers also get derailed. Because women characteristically place a high premium on relatedness, we often ignore or casually overrun the line between professional responsibilities and personal relationships. When a conversation with a supervisor over morning coffee about your love life is followed by a dressing-down after lunch because you've lost an important account or dropped the numbers on a budget spreadsheet, you may feel personally betrayed: how could someone with whom you've just shared the most intimate details of your life treat you so badly?

Confusing necessary criticism with a personal attack is a mistake many women often make. Says Reinhold, "Honest feedback is the scarcest commodity in the workplace today, especially in female-dominant organizations." And when personal friendships extend past office hours, it's even scarcer, which is why it's so necessary to protect your relationship as well as your job by confronting the potential problems before they affect either. Before the friendship ripens into real intimacy, it might be wise to tell the other person that although you have a lot in common besides your jobs, and in other circumstances you'd want to be good pals, spending a lot of time together outside the office might not be a great idea. But if you do pursue the friendship, it's essential to make some boundaries explicit rather than assume they're mutually understood; for instance, agreeing that you'll keep each other's personal secrets and not share professional ones; downplaying your friendship in the office so it doesn't alienate or exclude other colleagues; and avoiding obsessing about your job in your personal time together, and vice versa.

Many career professionals believe friendships that begin at work should be limited to that arena—that it's healthier to build your social structure outside the office. Says Reinhold, "The job isn't a place to get your affiliative needs met. Mixing social and office relationships muddies the waters, especially if you aspire to management. Professional evaluation—getting and giving critical as well as positive feedback—is difficult between intimates, and a supervisor's friendship is never unconditional." Research into blended relationships where friends are work associates highlights the conflicts that attend such balancing acts: equality versus inequality, impartiality versus favoritism, judgment versus acceptance, and openness versus closedness. The more formalized the organizational environment, the greater the dual-role tension and the less close the personal relationship, but those friends with unequal status were more able to manage the tension than dyads in which status in the organization was roughly equal!

Yet, as the writer Letty Pogrebin points out, work can often lead to some of life's most satisfying friendships; even coworkers who are not very close can constitute an extended family of sorts, and longevity can approximate closeness. Work can make friendship easier, and friendship can make even a bad job tolerable.

If your boundary style isn't somewhat flexible, you may find it difficult to take criticism of your work or professional behavior from someone you think of as a friend and perceive her comments as insensitive or unfair. It will take all your boundary intelligence to respond in the moment rather than taking it personally and letting hurt feelings fester. But using messages like "When you do or say A, it makes me feel B, which results in C" will help you get better feedback and clarify what's expected of you, as well as keeping a friendship that goes beyond the office from getting in the way of a positive professional relationship.

Needy, Greedy, Eat-Your-Life Bosses, and Other Office Hazards

The pseudointimacy some employers demand may reflect their need for control and/or the barrenness or difficulties in their personal lives. Even if your work/life boundary is pretty permeable, you may have to strengthen it to cope with their repeated invasions of your life off the clock. Mimi had a boss like that: "She called me at home, usually late on Saturdays, just to chat. She wanted to know if I had 'plans' for the evening and what they were. Or she'd outline this whole agenda for me; tell me what movies to see or books I should be reading. Or she'd say, if you're not busy this weekend, perhaps you could use the time to think about how we're going to pitch that new account. She made it very clear that I needed to be available to her at all times. Once she called me on a Sunday morning to say she was having some people over for brunch, could I possibly pick something up from a bakery and bring it over; another time, her daughter had a school play when she was out of town and she asked me if I'd go in her place, even though I didn't even know the girl!"

Mimi eventually quit her job with the overbearing boss, and when she interviewed for her next one, she asked for clarification about whether availability in her off hours, except in a real emergency, was expected of her. "I want to be successful in this company, and I'll work very hard to accomplish that. But I'm going to school at night, and I need evenings and weekends to study. Is that going to be a problem?"

Drea makes herself unavailable after hours—she has an unlisted home phone number, and voice mail and caller ID screen calls from her domineering boss during her personal time. Brenda asks her manager to e-mail her or leave a message on her office line when something comes up after hours that he deems critical, and she promises to give it first priority the next morning. But when these kinds of strategies fail and your work overruns your life, you may have to resign yourself to tell your superiors tactfully but clearly that making demands on you when you're involved in other things compromises your ability to give your job your full attention and prevents you from recharging your batteries off-hours so you can do your best work from nine to five.

In some jobs, being on call even during personal time or working way past normal hours comes with the territory. Marilyn, an associate at a law firm, knows that she's expected to put in eighty hours a week if she hopes to make partner. Tina, a TV reporter, understands that breaking news takes precedence over her plans for the evening. Beth, a pediatrician, tries to return all calls from worried parents before she leaves the clinic, but she also knows that kids get sick and parents get scared without regard for the doctor's schedule. But in the case of bosses who think your personal life is theirs to invade at their pleasure, suffering repeated intrusions on it makes you a patsy for continued punishment and takes its toll on both sides of the life/work boundary.

Dishing the Dirt vs. Sweeping It
Under the Rug

The line between people's work and their personal lives is often crossed at the watercooler. "When people discuss really private stuff—about themselves or others—I'm extremely uncomfortable," says Maddy, a middle manager at an insurance company, whose boundary style is in the middle range in permeability but high in flexibility. "I want to walk away, but I don't want to seem like a conceited bitch or cut myself off from information that might be important." When the talk gets raw or the gossip gets out of control, she changes the subject or tries to inject some humor into the situation to establish a more appropriate boundary. "Tossing in a ridiculous non sequitur like "Do you think the rain will hurt the rhubarb?' makes that point better than saying 'I think you're really out of line,'" she says. And when someone asks Theresa an intrusive personal question, "I do what my shrink does—answer it with a question of my own, even if I have to pretend to be interested in the answer." In other words, "Don't you think the ladies' room needs repainting?" is an appropriate response to "Are you sleeping with that fellow you were having lunch with yesterday?"—one that provides a reasonable balance between distance and closeness.

You needn't and shouldn't spill all the details of your life outside the office, but being open about the things most people who work together know about one another humanizes you so you don't get a reputation as being cold or standoffish. Rigid and impermeable boundaries that wall off every aspect of your personal life put you at a social and professional disadvantage; it's smarter to allude in passing to the fact that you have one, with some harmless disclosure. And when you have to tell someone at work things you'd rather no one else know—about medical or emotional problems for which you're making a claim on your health insurance, or a personal situation that impacts your performance, for example—establish the boundary by thanking your boss or the benefits manager in advance for protecting your privacy.

When Inside Information Isn't— and When It Should Be

When you're privy to knowledge that may affect your colleagues— for example, when Jackie learned that downsizing was in the works, or Gwen heard from her boss that her close friend Roseanne was going to lose her job if she didn't shape up—the fastest way to lose your own job is to pass it on, unless you've been asked directly by your boss to do so. Jackie negotiated that boundary crossing by telling her coworkers that given the uncertainty about the company's plans, she wasn't planning on making any major expenditures like buying a new car. Gwen didn't repeat what she'd heard about her friend's lagging performance but asked Roseanne if she minded if she offered some suggestions about how her work could be improved. Roseanne agreed—she took Gwen's constructive criticism in the spirit it was offered, and her "shape up" was soon apparent to her supervisors. But if she'd said, "As a matter of fact, I don't want your opinions," Gwen at least would have had the consolation of knowing she'd made a good attempt at heading off the problems that Roseanne didn't realize were jeopardizing her job.

If you know something about a colleague that directly affects the organization or impacts that person's ability to do his or her job—a drug or an alcohol problem, a threatening spouse, or suspected illegal activity—state your awareness of the situation to the person involved and be generous with your empathy, but limit your offer to help to the professional arena—you're not the Red Cross or the intervention specialist. If you decide that you must tell a supervisor, inform your colleague in advance of your intention. And if it's your boss who has the problem, don't go over his or her head unless it's the only option—even if it is, it may cost you your job, too.

When your values or ethics are compromised by your job, maintaining the boundary between your work and your life is difficult; the more permeable your boundary style is, the more difficult the dilemma you face. But quitting in a morally superior huff isn't always the best or the only way to proceed. Expressing your concerns to your superior might clarify matters; it could be that you've misinterpreted the situation and aren't being asked to do something that violates your principles. If you are, ask for an assignment to a different project or department, explaining your qualms without being judgmental. Here's where an "I" message such as "I don't feel comfortable doing that" is useful. Ethical conflicts aren't unusual, particularly in the health-care field; with the restrictions imposed by managed-care organizations that may compromise a caregiver's commitment to service, and the moral qualms posed by issues like abortion and the care of the terminally ill, many people are questioning whether they can continue in their profession and still remain true to their deeply held beliefs. Gail was deeply disturbed every time she had to deny coverage to someone for a procedure or other medical intervention deemed risky or inappropriate—or even too costly—by her employer, a health insurance company. "There was a woman with advanced breast cancer who might have survived with a bone marrow transplant, which the company didn't cover. I talked to her husband so many times I felt like I knew him. My own sister had breast cancer, and her policy covered the transplant—she's alive and healthy today, and that other woman's not. There was a woman who'd been badly beaten by her boyfriend, and while we paid for hospitalization and basic repair, she really needed a good plastic surgeon, but my boss said it was elective and cosmetic and made me turn her down. Finally I couldn't take it anymore—I quit."

Being aware of the boundary issues posed by the intersection of your job and the rest of your life—especially when working relationships are also personal ones—makes sense in both places. It allows you to get and give honest feedback, be part of a team without endangering meaningful friendships that give texture to your life in and out of the office, and handle competition and confrontation in a professional manner. Knowing where to draw the line makes it possible to feel safe instead of vulnerable on the job, maintain your focus while doing it, and be true to your ethical values. It makes you more productive in your career, refreshed in mind, body, and spirit outside it, and able to find real intimacy in your private life as well as true collegiality at work.

While interpersonal boundaries determine where on the relatedness continuum you connect with the social surround—the many people you encounter every day on a nonintimate basis—organizational boundaries have to do with the culture, norms, and practices of the work environment, which is where many cases of boundary misfit occur. In organizational, technological, and administrative fields, from law to finance to the corporate world, certain role-defined and procedural boundaries are built into the work. Some are formally spelled out in the employee manual, specified by administrative edict, or established by common understanding or practice. The boundary issues generated by and in the working environment aren't the same as those that separate your work from the rest of your life, although they are related in terms of permeability and complexity. Here is a quiz that's directly related to organizational boundaries and how your boundary style complements or conflicts with them.

Organizational/Personal Boundary Style Quiz

Please read each answer key before responding as some answers are different or reverse-scored.

1. Everyone in an organization should have specific
   roles and responsibilities.   _____
   1 = true   2 = often true   3 = sometimes true
   4 = never true

2. I'd rather follow rules and procedures than make them up as the situation requires or operate according to my own. _____

   1 = true   2 = often true   3 = sometimes true
   4 = never true

3. It's difficult for me to work with people who are very different from me. _____

   1 = true   2 = often true   3 = sometimes true
   4 = never true

4. I'm very frank in the office about how I feel about my bosses, employees, the company, and my job. _____

   1 = never   2 = sometimes   3 = often   4 = always

5. The process of accomplishing a professional goal is as important as the result. _____

   1 = never   2 = sometimes   3 = often   4 = always

6. I have a hard time working with people who second-guess me or question my decisions. _____

   1 = always   2 = often   3 = sometimes   4 = never

7. I prefer to work on things I enjoy doing before tackling less pleasant or interesting tasks. _____

   1 = never   2 = occasionally   3 = often   4 = always

8. I avoid playing office politics, even when it could affect my own position or advancement. _____

   1 = never true   2 = sometimes true   3 = often true
   4 = always true

9. I wouldn't work for a company whose values or policies weren't in line with my own. _____

   1 = not true   2 = sometimes true   3 = often true
   4 = always true

10. The most important thing about my job is my
     paycheck.   _____
     1 = true   2 = often true   3 = sometimes true
     4 = never true

Total   _____

The higher your score on this quiz, the more likely it is that some
or all of the following adjectives describe your organizational
boundaries: unconventional, self-motivated, process-oriented, non-
analytic, antiauthoritarian, noncompetitive, experiential, and emotional. If those qualities aren't seen as a plus by your organization,
you might be happier and more productive in another one.

You and the Corporate Culture— Good Fit or Misfit?

There are many ways of describing an organization's culture, and
this book can't begin to do justice to the extensive research on the
subject. But it's important to realize that your boundaries and those
of your workplace interact according to where you are in the corporate hierarchy, which is the organizing principle for most businesses.

Organizational boundaries reflect how organizations allocate
responsibility, power, and authority; restrict or reward initiative; recognize individual as well as collective achievement; and promote or
limit information, participation, and self-management. They indicate whether the culture of the workplace is formal and hierarchical
or casual and expressive; task, title, or role defined; profit or mission
driven; collaborative or competitive; service, process, or product oriented; and inward or outward looking. And they represent the
guiding ethos of the organization—where it is on the continuum
from punitive to empowered or open to closed. As the organizational psychologist Jack Gibb writes, an important dimension of the

environment is the level of trust expressed by its boundaries, which describe how authentically ourselves they permit or encourage us to be, and how adaptive and responsive they are to our intrinsic as well as extrinsic needs—in other words, how rigid or permeable the organization's boundaries are.

Analyzing the boundary culture of your organization is key to determining whether it brings out the best in you. If it conflicts with your boundary style more than it conforms to it, and if that mismatch is difficult to tolerate despite the pay, perks, and promotions it promises, burnout isn't just likely—it's highly probable. From an employer's perspective, goodness of fit means how suited you are to the job or task for which you're hired. From yours, though, goodness of fit has a wider meaning. Does your work support your psychological as well as professional development? Do its structure and processes foster your creativity? Does your job require you to act in ways that are congruent with your values? Does it leverage your professional strengths or minimize them, honor or exploit your loyalty to the organization, stifle or engage your initiative?

Your overall boundary permeability as well as your answers on the preceding quiz probably reflect the fit or misfit between the kind of work you're doing and the culture you do it in. If your boundaries score in the middle or low range on permeability, you may be better suited to working in an organization with established group norms and expectations than in a less structured one. For example, Shannon's score on the organizational quiz was relatively high in permeability—not surprising in a self-described free spirit who has little patience with the rules, procedures, and role stratification that govern her day-to-day work as a sales and marketing manager in a Fortune 500 company. While it's her creativity and vision that her employer values, her impatience with "going through channels," disregard for what she calls "the tyranny of the organization chart," penchant for speaking her mind at work regardless of the political consequences, and especially her difficulty in controlling her emotions in the office have kept her from advancing up the corporate ladder. She'd probably be happier working on her own or in a smaller, less hierarchical company, but so far she hasn't found a way to do that and still afford health insurance.

Like Shannon, Margaret works for a highly stratified corporation that lives and dies according to its organization chart. Also like Shannon, she tends to speak her mind, lose her cool in highly charged situations with coworkers, and "color outside the lines," which often means ignoring established procedures. Her real talent is as a catalyst rather than a manager, yet in her job, managerial skills count more than vision. A year ago she went out on her own as a coach and consultant—interestingly enough, most of her business thus far comes from the very company that refused to put her on the management track. "They want what I have to offer, they just didn't want to deal with who I am," Margaret says. "The corporate bandwidth here is much narrower than it is at other places—there's just so much a conservative, traditional, always-done-it-this-way company like this can tolerate without turning the system upside down, which of course is what has to happen if we're going to be competitive in the industry." Yet Margaret spent fifteen years there in an often-frustrating situation she describes as "always pushing a rock uphill." She stayed, she says, "because they needed me—their expressed goal was to change the corporate culture, and that's my expertise. Unfortunately, they weren't really committed to doing it." Still, enough of the company's departments and subsidiaries have hired her back as a consultant, which gratifies her: "It means they recognize *my ability*, regardless of the fact that they're not comfortable with my style. What I do is fire people up and help them clarify their vision—I rock the boat. But ultimately they're the ones who have to ride in it . . . if they don't want to, they're wasting their money and my time."

Alicia is an account executive in a much more free-wheeling public relations agency, yet as her scores on both the work/life and organizational boundary quizzes indicate, she might be more satisfied in Margaret's or Shannon's professional environment. Unlike most of her colleagues, Alicia keeps her personal life very separate from her work—her closest colleagues had no idea she even had children until a school emergency made them aware of it. She's uncomfortable with an office in which "everyone knows everyone else's business, people ignore the rules, do their own thing, and spend as much time making sure everyone's happy and feels heard than getting out the work on time."

Katrina is a programmer at a company that makes video games, which means "working with a bunch of teenage boys—or men who act that way." Although her work is a pretty solitary pursuit, at her company it takes place in a "bullpen" where Nerf balls and empty soda cans often whiz right over her monitor and even the mandatory headphones don't drown out the steady hum of hard rock music. Employees are encouraged to work around the clock, which doesn't fit in with Katrina's responsibilities to her partner and child or her commitments to the environmental group she chairs. "The team ethos is very strong here, and the testosterone level quite high," she says. She's never brought her lesbian partner to a company function—"They say they're committed to diversity, but if I were 'out' at work, I'd never hear the end of the dirty jokes," she comments. Although her score on the work/life boundary quiz (page 184) was in the low permeable range, it was closer to the middle in the organizational/personal boundary style quiz (page 195); her overall boundary style, though, is much more permeable, reflecting her openness to inner experience, intimacy with her partner and friends, and generally positive attitude toward other people. Not surprisingly, she's acutely aware that she doesn't "fit in" at work and wishes she could pursue her vocation in a different environment. "I have this fantasy of an all-woman company where we shared ourselves as well as our skills," she said. "Where there was a better balance between working alone and working in teams. Where human qualities like empathy, mutuality, and caring weren't seen as a distraction from work but an aspect of it. Unfortunately, that's not what happens at most technology companies, and that's where my professional skills are valuable."

Triangulating the Boundaries—
Pitfall or Policy?

Interpersonal trust and cooperation are important for technology collaborations as well as client professional service firm relationships, comarketing alliances, and other partnerships with goals related to producing and/or sharing knowledge; in such contexts, the risk of opportunism is high, and performance often depends on the ability of employees to cooperate effectively across organizational boundaries. But misaligned goals and assumptions can sidetrack this process; so, too, can the nature of the organizational boundaries and the procedures that reflect them. At the manufacturing company where Marcy works, each department is its own little fiefdom, and when the task calls for mutual cooperation and teamwork, loyalties and alliances to one's own group are often tested. Marcy cites the example of working with several other people in a boundary-crossing team where two people from different organizations within the company had difficulty working together. "The friction between them was sabotaging the project and fragmenting the team," she says. "But instead of working it out between themselves, or even going to the team manager for help in resolving their differences, they each went to their own individual managers, like two kids playing Mommy and Daddy off each other." That's par for the course at her company, where "direct reports" are often just the opposite. In some organizations, this kind of triangulation isn't necessarily spelled out in the employee manual, but it's an aspect of the cultural norms, and employees deviate from it at their peril.

Using boundary intelligence to manage your inner boundaries by increasing their permeability enough to imagine another's thoughts or feelings from that person's point of view can facilitate cooperation across boundaries. So can decreasing it enough to avoid the trap of organizational triangles or other dysfunctional coalitions. The more complex your boundaries are, the better you'll be at negotiating how power, proximity, and interest are allocated and knowledge, information, and other resources are shared when organizational boundaries are crossed.

Boundaries are interfaces between the organization and its environment, and the most critical component of the environment is the human one. Organizational boundaries are a semipermeable membrane that protects the organization from much of the uncertainty in the environment; without them, the organization would be wholly unpredictable and unorganized. How you relate to the boundary culture of your organization and environment—how your boundary style fits with it—may not be the most important factor in job satisfaction or even performance. But it's an important consideration in deciding whether your work increases your sense of personal efficacy, satisfies your needs for intellectual stimulation, challenge, creativity, community, and an adequate standard of living, and whether it provides at least as much balance between the personal and the professional as you need (if not as much as you want).

CHAPTER 11

When Boundary Styles Collide

Your breathing gets shallow. Your heart races. Your muscles tense up. Your gut tightens. You grind your teeth. Your mouth dries up. Your hands feel clammy and cold. Your forehead perspires. Your head hurts. Your pupils dilate. Your eyes twitch. You have to go to the bathroom.

And that's just what happens in the *first* stage of generalized arousal syndrome (also known as the fight-or-flight response), which occurs whenever emotional trespass threatens or boundary styles collide. The physiological changes of GAS (yes, that may happen, too!) result from the body's chemical and hormonal reactions to danger—real or perceived. But when the danger is psychological rather than physical, how you think, feel, and act changes, too. You're hypervigilant, on the alert for further attack or the conflict to come. You're overly sensitive—all your emotions are in a heightened state of arousal, so that a word, a gesture, a memory, or even a nudge to your unconscious can trigger a reaction, change your mind, or set you off. You're obsessive—you rehearse or play back the conversation, comment, or incident that triggered the arousal, think over what was said or done, get down on yourself for not being fast enough with the right comeback. You're irritable and cranky, not just with whoever injured you but with anyone in your range. And you're wrung out and exhausted, no matter how much sleep you had last night.

In this state, everything you communicate, do, perceive, feel, remember, and learn is governed by fear, anger, or anxiety. Since an argument (or even the anticipation of one) with a friend, a lover, a family member, or an office mate isn't usually a life-threatening experience, all those bodily changes mobilized by the generalized arousal syndrome take a physical as well as an emotional toll, sending your stress level skyward. So learning how to redefine conflict so it doesn't send your system a "danger" message when there's no saber-toothed tiger lurking outside your cave isn't just a better way to handle it when it comes up in your relationships—which it always does—but is healthier, too. It turns off the alarm from the amygdala, or emotional brain, allowing your neocortex to analyze what just happened (or is about to) and process its higher levels of meaning; not just its transactional content—what you said, what he did—but also how it reflects or affects the relationship itself.

What's This Fight Really About?

Couples fight about money, sex, parenting, decision making, family, friends, work, time, and who's responsible for everything from sorting the laundry to walking the dog. Mary and Duke bicker about their in-laws—she thinks his mother's intrusive and overbearing, he disapproves of her gay brother's lifestyle and won't permit their sons to be alone with him. Jacy and Chet argue about his weekly poker game—she won't have it at their house because she can't rid the house of the cigar smoke for days—and her former roommate, whom he dated briefly before they were married. Blake and Ariel can't talk politics without a blowup—she's an ardent Democrat, and he thinks her political pals are flakes and nuts.

Parents and children (grown or not) fight about whose life it is, who owes whom, who's right about values, beliefs, and lifestyles, which sibling got the most or the least, and whose story of what happened a long time ago (or even yesterday) is accurate. Mona and her mother can't spend ten minutes together without one of them breaking into tears—Mona thinks her mother demands too much of her time, and Isabelle thinks her daughter is selfish and ungracious. Dolly and her father have vastly different recollections of many events in her childhood—especially how harsh, rigid, and emotionally abusive he was, which Jack remembers as "what a parent does to raise a responsible kid." Tory's mother has never forgiven her for moving a thousand miles away instead of staying closer, where she could help out with her ailing father and younger sister. Lorna won't talk to her son-in-law because he's not Jewish or come to her grandchild's confirmation.

Friends fight about other friends and lovers, time, loyalty, money, ideas, values, and choices; whose turn it is to drive, pay, choose, decide, or apologize; and whether the friendship is worth the trouble. Dee and Lexy play a game of one-upmanship that expresses the competitiveness they can't acknowledge—whether it's men, money, or who's a better bridge player, there's always an undercurrent of tension in their relationship. Grace is jealous of Bridget's friendship with a woman she doesn't like, and Bridget punishes Grace for her possessiveness by not calling her back for several days after Grace leaves a message on her machine.

Colleagues fight about authority, responsibility, recognition, equality, and turf—who has it, who ought to, and who shouldn't. Steffie and Pat, who run a family business, argue about who's in charge of what, when each takes her vacation, and which of them should represent the company in public. Antonia and Melanie squabble about who's in charge of their team, and Barbara and Nikki jockey for position so publicly that their boss often has to reprimand them. And Gina's colleagues routinely disparage her contributions, despite how good they are. "It's because I'm almost twenty years older than most of them—they treat me like I'm their mother, which is to say they're very patronizing." It's not age discrimination in a legal sense, she says "but in terms of our working relationship, it sure feels like it."

But that's not all these fights are about. Most conflicts, in most relationships, are also about boundaries—claiming, clarifying, defending, and maintaining them. So boundary style and boundary intelligence have as much if not more to do with how you deal with conflict than with who's right or wrong.

As Long As We're Fighting, We're Alive!

All conflicts have these two dimensions of meaning—the transactional and the relational—and boundary style influences both. It determines how you act or react—whether and how you advance or retreat, ignore or respond, reach out for connection or strive for greater distance. The capacity to respond to conflict in both its dimensions is closely correlated to boundary intelligence, which requires the ability to see the relationship in multiple time frames— in the past and the future as well as the present—in order to manage your boundaries effectively in all of them. This perspective enables you to sort out the interests, values, preferences, realities, and emotional investments that are driving the conflict, acknowledge which are yours and which are the other person's, and assume that it's possible to satisfy at least some of both . . . if not in this moment, then at a future point in the relationship.

When Conflict Brings You Closer

There are plenty of good, strong, resilient relationships where conflict seems to energize both participants to greater closeness. "It's how we communicate," says Rose, who admits that "it keeps everything moving because it makes us stop and really notice or listen or see each other, which you don't usually do once a relationship is established because you think you know everything about the person." "It puts things into perspective and makes you realize what's really important," says Geila. "It forces you to think about whether your own position is really solid or just a knee-jerk reaction," says Courtney. "It's how you know the relationship is vital and alive, not stagnant and superficial," says Marianne.

Sophie and Dace's friendship has lasted through "three noisy decades," as Dace describes them, adding "and not all of the noise has been laughter, either." On several occasions over the years, their conflicts have estranged these two friends from each other for months. "We used to joke that we were like this couple that kept getting divorced from each other and then remarrying," says Sophie of their extended periods of separation. They're both sensitive, emotionally responsive women whose boundary style maps are remarkably similar, only a single digit apart in overall permeability (high) and exactly the same in variability (low-medium) and complexity (high). "When she says something callous or hurtful, I really take it to heart," says Sophie, "although less than I used to." Says Dace, "When she criticizes me, it wounds me like a knife."

Yet because their boundaries are complex enough—and because the relationship is equally important to both of them—during those periods they strive for connection on other, less intimate levels. "Maybe we had a fight because one of us hit a sore spot in the other, you know, pushed some button, and we won't talk to each other for a couple of days. But then we'll just sort of table it and go to the movies or shopping or have our nails done together . . . something that doesn't involve a lot of 'processing.' Later we might go back to what happened, or just ignore it until it happens again, or maybe twice more. So then we'll have these, like, concrete examples of how one of us discounted the other one's opinions or did something hurtful. That's when we'll deal with it, not just in terms of what happened right then, but what it means in terms of our whole friendship," says Dace. "But conflict is how we change and grow, and we always come out of it feeling more together as well as more aware of the fact that we're separate people." In other words, the energy created by their frequent conflicts promotes constructive rather than destructive change in their relationship, allowing them the separateness they need as well as the connectedness to which they're committed.

When Conflict Drives You Apart

Connie and her father have dinner together at his club once a month, an occasion she used to enjoy. But her father's admission that he's having an affair and his repetitious recounting of all the ways her mother drove him to it have made the evenings uncomfortable for her, and now she looks for reasons to avoid him and her mother as well. "I feel like a fraud when we're together because I know something about their marriage that she doesn't," she says. "I feel like a traitor to my own values by not telling him that unless he tells Mom, I'm going to."

Tyra is the treasurer of a family-owned business; her brother, Will, is in charge of purchasing. She knows he's getting payoffs from his suppliers—"He calls them 'sweeteners,' says everybody does it, and tells me I'm naive to think otherwise." Her father's succession plans call for both Tyra and Will to take over the company when he retires, as CFO and CEO, respectively. "Maybe Will's right, I am naive. But it's not something I want to be part of," says Tyra. "Which means that when Dad retires or dies and we take over, there'll be a knock-down, drag-out fight that only one of us can win. It will be the end of my relationship with Will, and it'll kill my Mom, too."

Tiffany's parents had no clue she was lesbian until she came out to them at age twenty-eight. "First they gulped, then they told me it was a phase I was going through, and then they accepted it . . . sort of. But they never stop criticizing Macy, my partner. We've been together for five years, and while they're polite when they're with us, as soon as she's out of hearing—and sometimes when she isn't—

they make some bitchy comment about what she's wearing or how she doesn't treat me well enough. And they still haven't stopped trying to fix me up with their friends' sons. They keep saying, give him a chance, you never know." She's tried steeling herself when they do it. "We end up fighting about something else . . . why I didn't dry the wineglasses before I put them away, why I forgot my sister's birthday, stuff like that. But I know what it's really about—their continued denial of who I really am. And when I confront them with that, they just say, 'Oh, darling, you see everything through lavender glasses, it has nothing to do with your 'friend,'" Tiffany says.

Stacy, Nikki, and Jen have been friends since they were college roommates, and Nikki's been in the middle ever since. "If Jen's mad at Stacy, she replays the whole argument to me, expecting to hear me say, you're right and she's wrong; if I don't, she accuses me of being disloyal to her. If Jen doesn't tell Stacy something she tells me, and Stacy finds out about it later, she gets pissed off at both of us, especially me. I can't win, and I'm tired of being the referee; I've asked them both to stop, and it works for a while, but then they're at it again. Lately I've been dodging their phone calls and feeling like a wuss for not telling them why. I miss them both, but I don't miss the aggravation."

The Difference between Resolving Conflict and Transforming It

Problem-solving conflict resolution resolves specific short-term difficulties, while usually ignoring or avoiding long-term relationship issues. But transforming conflict with boundary intelligence goes beyond the immediate situation to alter the way in which you view your relationship—the meaning you make of it—as well as how you treat one another.

For Tyra, telling her father what's going on and/or demanding that Will stop doing it or she'll leave the company might solve the immediate problem, but it may have serious repercussions in her entire family: "Maybe Dad knows what's going on and condones it—what'll I do then?" she wonders. But enlarging the context of the conflict by bringing up the subject of supplier payoffs in general— without pointing fingers at whether they're happening in their company—is a better way to clarify the company's values and also make her own. If her father and brother see nothing wrong with the practice, and she can't persuade them that the legal and ethical consequences outweigh any short-term personal financial gain, she may have to leave the family business and even endure some emotional distance from her father and brother for a while. But if she can shift her focus from what divides them to what still connects them—the touch football games after church on Sunday, the birth of the newest grandchild, concern for an elderly relative's declining health, the annual family ski trip—she can preserve her relationships with her family and even expand them, since according to her, "the family business often seems like all we ever talk about."

Connie's immediate dilemma might be resolved by bringing her father's affair out in the open, but it's certain to have long-lasting negative repercussions on her relationship with both of her parents. Dealing with it two dimensionally requires restating the boundaries that are being ignored (her own as well as her parents' marital boundary) and pointing out the consequences that this will have on all their relationships over time: "Dad, this is between you and Mom, not you and me. It's not my problem, and I can't solve it . . . only you and she can, and you may need a counselor to help you. If you don't know one, maybe I can help you find somebody. When you talk about Mom, it makes me feel sad for her and want to avoid her. When you try to justify what you're doing by telling me it's her fault, it makes me angry and disappointed in you and makes me want to avoid you. So I'm not going to listen any longer, and unless you stop talking about it, I'm leaving, and I'll only see you and Mom together, not separately."

Tiffany believes her frequent clashes with her parents are about her lesbianism, and that may be true. But responding only in terms of the present problem might be a better strategy for their entire relationship than seeing every conflict as an example of her parents' inability to fully accept her sexual preference. "I always air-dry my wineglasses so they won't streak, but if you want me to do it your way in your house, I'll be glad to," or "Thanks for reminding me about Shay's birthday, I'd totally spaced it—I'll call her today and apologize and see if I can take her out for dinner next week when things aren't so crazy at the office" doesn't deal with their disapproval of her sexual orientation, but she can't make them change that; she can only change the way she responds to it, and one way to do that is ignore it as well as she can. In fact, her mother's advice isn't all bad—it might help her to stop looking at every conflict as a referendum on her sexuality and only deal directly with it when it occurs by telling her parents that she is who she is, she'd like them to accept it, and if they can't, that's their problem and not hers.

Nikki needs to point out to Stacy and Jen what their constant triangulation is doing to their long-term friendship. In addition to responding in the moment when one of them does it—a firm "Take this up with her, not me; let's talk about something else"—she might ask both of them to lunch together and explain why she's been avoiding them, how their behavior affects her, and what the consequences will be if they keep putting her in the middle: "I'll just stop seeing both of you, which will make me very sad, and I don't think it'll make the two of you very happy, either."

How Boundary Style Shapes Your Response to Conflict

Boundary style isn't determined by boundary intelligence, but it is related to how you deal with conflict; the more permeable your inner boundaries are, for example, the harder you may find it to separate your thoughts from your emotions. So while someone is telling you something your mind knows is valid or true (*Yes, I did forget to pay the insurance premium*), you can't distinguish the message from your feelings about it (*I'm not only incompetent, I put our entire financial future at risk . . . and besides, what would I do if you died?*).

Conversely, the less permeable your interpersonal boundaries are, the more difficult it may be for you to be tactful and considerate of another person's feelings in an argument, the more likely you are to ignore rather than notice conflict in a relationship, and the less satisfied you are with compromising, even when either or both tactics might improve the relationship—if not right now, then over the long term.

Conflict, like boundaries, is dialectical in nature, a back-and-forth process that regulates closeness and distance from moment to moment in every interaction. That's why each person's boundary style influences what happens when it occurs.

June's boundary style is more permeable than flexible; her husband Bill's style is much less permeable than hers but somewhat more flexible. Thus he's able to open up or limit his permeability more easily than she can, even though his range is more limited. So although they eventually kiss and make up after an argument, his hurtful words play in her head long after he's fallen asleep; she lies awake wondering, Am I really that (*cold, unattractive, bitchy, dumb, pigheaded?*) while he snores on, since his greater flexibility allowed him to shut out her own equally negative personal comments; they've left barely a mark on his self-esteem.

Cheryl's boundary style is moderately permeable overall; her intimate boundaries are more permeable than her inner or interpersonal ones, reflecting her marriage to a man she describes as "my other half—really!" She's also an analytic person who doesn't let her emotions influence her, especially at the office. Nicole, who reports to her, is a somewhat disorganized but highly creative woman, described by Cheryl as "the most talented person I've ever supervised." But Nicole is also the bane of Cheryl's existence: "She's always late with her work, she ignores the procedures I've set up to make sure no mistakes get through, and she's somewhat of an icon-oclast who thinks rules were made for everyone but her. When the heat's on, she always comes through, usually with a brilliant solution to a problem that has everyone else stumped, but she puts so much stress on the rest of the group that I'm often tempted to fire her. I'd really hate to let her go—not just because other agencies would jump at the chance to hire her, but because I think it would undermine my own performance rating; my boss would think I wasn't a good enough manager to handle her." Needless to say, Nicole's boundary style is much higher in permeability and lower in both flexibility and complexity than Cheryl's; the same qualities that account for her creativity also limit her ability to focus on the task at hand, follow office procedures, and keep her emotional volatility from distracting her colleagues.

Dina's relationship with her teenage daughter has always been the envy of all her friends, especially those with difficult and rebellious adolescents of their own. "Kira used to tell me everything," Dina says sadly. "We were each other's best friends." While it's normal (and necessary) for teenagers to claim their autonomy and separate emotionally from their parents, it's particularly difficult to do so when that developmental step is seen as abandonment, as it is by Dina, whose own mother was a distant, aloof parent who was always "just out of reach," as Dina describes her. So is her husband. When she says, "I always thought if I just loved him enough, he'd open up," it's easy to see that she's talking about Kira as well as Jason. Dina's boundaries are much more permeable than theirs, which is why their emotional cutoff—a defense against her attempts to "colonize" their thoughts and feelings—is so painful to her. As Kira explains, "Like we have this constant battle about why I don't go to church with her anymore," she says. "And when I say it's because I don't believe all that crap and she tells me I'm wrong, I don't know what I believe. If I say I don't eat meat, I'm a vegetarian, she starts in about how ridiculous that is, I wear leather shoes, don't I? If I tell her I'm pissed off at my sister, she says, No, you're not, you really love her. If I tell her I'm hungry, she says, You can't be, you just ate. If she's in a bad mood and I'm in a good one, it's like I'm being disloyal just by feeling happy . . . I have to get away from her before she brings me down."

Kira's boundary style is still somewhat fluid, given her tender age, but she's already beginning to thicken not only her intimate boundaries but her interpersonal ones, too. She's become extremely close-mouthed about her feelings, thoughts, and behavior with her friends, teachers, and siblings as well as her mother. "Give someone an inch and they'll take a mile," she says off-handedly. "You're better off if you don't get too close to anyone, because if you do, you just disappear."

It's not only differences in boundary styles that engender conflict; as we saw with Sophie and Dace, similarities can cause problems, too, especially when permeability is high and flexibility is low.

Using the Basic Skills of Boundary Intelligence to Cope with Conflict

Regardless of how permeable your boundaries are, their flexibility and complexity are more important influences on how you deal with conflict or confrontation. Varying your permeability keeps personal attacks from damaging your sense of self or taking up residence in it, while simultaneously letting in information about the other person's feelings, thoughts, beliefs, values, and needs that might lead to a compromise or a solution as well as enlighten you about the underlying issues or differences that exist in the relationship.

Managing the complexity of your boundaries in the midst of conflict takes a high degree of boundary intelligence. It's what propels you to focus not just on the areas of disconnection or distance but also on those that exist for connection and closeness—if not in this moment, then in past and future ones. And it's also what makes it possible for you to take responsibility only for your part in the conflict, not the conflict itself, which turns it into something only both of you acting together can solve.

The basic skills of boundary intelligence—awareness, insight, intention, and action—are operating when you take conscious control of your boundaries by varying their permeability to avoid being drawn into a conflict whose unconscious goal is to satisfy the other person's psychological need. Recognizing someone else's projections of anger, self-doubt, or fear that are too painful for that person to feel or acknowledge herself and managing your own permeability so that those projections bounce off your psychological surround before they become part of you or of the conflict itself is using your boundary intelligence. (So is recognizing when the projections are coming from you.) It's boundary intelligence that enables you to contain your own negative feelings when they're stirred up in the heat of an argument, so that they inform but don't "contaminate" your response or take you over and provoke a misguided one.

Conflict Style Quiz

Here's a quiz to bring your conflict style into clearer focus. Please read each answer key carefully as some answers are different or reverse-scored.

1. When my lover says we need to talk, it's never
   a good sign.   _____
   1 = always true   2 = often true   3 = sometimes true
   4 = never true

2. Avoiding conflict is better for a relationship than
   engaging in it.   _____
   1 = always true   2 = often true   3 = sometimes true
   4 = never true

3. Once you concede something in an argument,
   you're at a disadvantage.   _____
   1 = always true   2 = often true   3 = sometimes true
   4 = never true

4. It's better for a relationship to leave little
   disagreements in an ambiguous state rather than
   resolve them.   _____
   1 = always true   2 = often true   3 = sometimes true
   4 = never true

5. I have trouble holding onto my own position in
   an argument.   _____
   1 = never true   2 = sometimes true   3 = often true
   4 = always true

6. I can feel close to someone even when we
   disagree.   _____
   1 = always true   2 = often true   3 = sometimes true
   4 = never true

7. Conflict is usually based on misunderstandings
   rather than real differences in facts, beliefs, values,
   or interests.   _____
   1 = never true   2 = sometimes true   3 = often true
   4 = always true

8. When I lose in a conflict or an argument, it feels
   like I've lost a part of myself.   _____
   1 = always true   2 = sometimes true   3 = often true
   4 = never true

9. I lose arguments or confrontations because I let
   my feelings get in the way of facts.   _____
   1 = never true   2 = sometimes true   3 = often true
   4 = always true

10. If you lose an argument or confrontation, it means
    the other person won.   _____

    1 = always true   2 = often true   3 = sometimes true
    4 = never true

Total   _____

Chances are, the higher your permeability and the lower your flexibility, the lower your score on this quiz will be. What's more important about these questions than your score, though, is the light they shed on how your boundary style influences how you deal with conflict.

Understanding how your boundary style affects how you feel about conflict and how you handle it is important, but getting a read on how others do—especially those with whom you're most often in conflict or disagreement—is just as important. So try taking the preceding quiz as if an adversary were taking it. For example, knowing that your adversary believes that giving any ground is the same as giving it all might change the way you frame your differences. Understanding that he or she has difficulty feeling close to someone who challenges his or her opinions or decisions might make you more willing to reach out for connection in another dimension of your relationship.

Using your boundary intelligence and employing your skills of awareness, insight, intention, and action can lead to the best and highest use of conflict; not reducing or resolving it or winning or losing, but transforming it into a reconciliation and reconfirmation of the "we" in the "I" that has room for both distance and connection.

Afterword

We cross boundaries every time we make a transition between our various roles and identities—parent, child, friend, lover, manager, employee, colleague, competitor, individual, and group member. We bump up against other people's boundaries and realize our own in the give and take and back and forthness of all our relationships, from the casual to the most important. Every boundary crossing, every meeting at the edge, is fraught with tension, but every one is also filled with possibilities—not only for improving the relationship but for getting more of what we want and less of what we don't and resolving that lifelong conflict between what often seem like opposing needs.

Getting both intimacy and independence in any one relationship isn't easy, especially when it's with a partner, a lover, a parent, a child, or a close friend. That's where boundary intelligence comes in. It's exercising a capacity you probably already have; its basic skill of awareness is well within range of anyone whose boundaries are permeable enough to recognize emotional trespass when it happens or react to that silent alarm that warns us it's about to. Insight, the next skill, doesn't take an in-depth knowledge of psychology or even a highly analytic mind; it's a matter of thinking about boundary events when they occur as expressions of someone's need or desire for more or less distance or closeness in the relationship—yours, his, or hers. Intention, the third skill, is a little more complicated; it requires that you decide not just what you want but figure out how to get it in a way that will help rather than hinder the relationship while also preserving your own integrity and authenticity. The more you know where your boundaries are and the better you know and are guided by your real self, the easier it is to master the fourth skill, action; managing the permeability, flexibility, and complexity of your boundaries to achieve your intention.

The paradox of inner boundaries is how stable they remain even though every new mental experience rearranges the meaning of previous ones and literally changes the mind. In the ongoing process that relationship *is*, it's boundary intelligence that rearranges the meaning of Me and Not Me and by doing so, changes who Me is, another example of the truism that the more we know others, in fact, the more we know ourselves.

We can only infer other people's boundary styles by what they say and how they act. The more closely we observe them from a boundary perspective, the more clearly we can see where, how, and whether our boundary style and theirs conflict or complement each other—with that understanding, we can use our boundary intelligence to improve how we manage ourselves in our relationship with them. Because we can only manage our own boundaries and our own part in the relationship. The more a part of our inner and relational life boundary intelligence is, the easier that will be. And the more likely it is that we can find in all our relationships the place where intimacy and autonomy, closeness and distance, can peacefully and authentically coexist.

Notes

Introduction

1 *But the psyche remembers* M. S. Mahler, F. Pine, and A. Bergman, *The Psychological Birth of the Human Infant* (New York: Basic Books, 1975).

9 *Boundaries are dynamic and fluid* Nancy Popp, *The Concept and Phenomenon of Psychological Boundaries from a Dialectical Perspective: An Empirical Exploration* (Ph.D. dissertation, Harvard University, 1993). A doctoral investigation that focuses on boundaries in relationships from a constructive developmental perspective.

Chapter 1. Boundary Basics: A Primer

18 *Is this something I hate? That hurts me?* Daniel Goleman, *Emotional Intelligence* (New York: Bantam Books, 1995). A cogent, accessible explanation of emotional intelligence first described by Howard Gardner.

19 *the loss of that common skin* Didier Anzieu, *Le moi-peau* (Paris: Monod Press, 1987).

20 *According to Dr. Ernest Hartmann* Ernest Hartmann, *Boundaries in the Mind: A New Psychology of Personality* (New York: Basic Books, 1991). Hartmann not only explains the phenomenology of boundaries but presents a boundary questionnaire that measures them in several different dimensions.

a normal sickness Donald Winnicott, *The Family and Individual Development* (London: Tavistock Publications, 1958).

24   *whether we* are *it or* have *it*   Robert Kegan, *The Evolving Self* (Cambridge, Mass.: Harvard University Press, 1982). A lucid and readable explanation of the stages of mental development from a constructive developmental perspective whose primary investigational instrument is the subject-object interview.

27   *attitudes toward time and money*   Hartmann, op. cit.

28   *a mental set or class with its own properties*   Kegan, op. cit.

      in some relation to each other   Popp, op. cit.

29   *a healthy insulation barrier*   Louis Ormond, "Developing Emotional Insulation," *International Journal of Group Psychotherapy* 44, no. 3 (1994).

32   *I don't make a huge distinction*   Letty Pogrebin, *Among Friends* (New York: McGraw-Hill, 1987).

35   *Once the realization is accepted*   R. M. Rilke, *Letters to a Young Poet* (New York: Norton, 1954).

Chapter 2. Emotional Trespass and Other Crimes of the Heart

38   *Because there are no public trials*   Leston Havens, *Learning to Be Human* (Reading, Mass.: Addison Wesley, 1994).

Chapter 3. What's Your Boundary Style?

46   *One of these researchers*   Hartmann, op. cit. Hartmann's Boundary Questionnaire was the starting point for the Boundary Style Questionnaire presented in this book, particularly the dimensions of emotional and intrapsychic boundaries. Other sources used in the construction of my questionnaire include the Measurement of Emotional Separation Scale (MES), the Miller Social Intimacy Scale, and the Intimacy Attitude Scale.

52   *Nancy Popp's research*   Popp, op. cit.

Chapter 4. Where Do Our Boundaries Come From?

75   *more than just a regressive replay*   Kegan, op. cit.

76   *There is no such thing as [just] an infant*   Donald Winnicott, *The Matura-*

tional Processes and the Facilitating Environment (New York: International Universities Press, 1965).

83   *Whose privacy did I violate?*   Judith Guest, *Ordinary People* (New York: Viking, 1976).

84   *How each of us views the world*   Judith Guest, *The Mythic Family* (Minneapolis: Milkweed Editions, 1988).

85   *One of the best literary allusions*   James Joyce, *A Portrait of the Artist as a Young Man* (New York: Viking, 1964).

89   *made our peace with heterosexual lust*   Judith Viorst, *Necessary Losses* (New York: Simon & Schuster, 1986).

Chapter 5. Family Whether We Like It or Not

92   *the multigenerational transmission process*   Murray Bowen, *Family Therory in Clinical Practice* (New York: Jason Aronson, 1978).

Chapter 6. The We of Me and Vice Versa

109   *the intimate edge in relatedness*   Darlene Ehrenberg, "The Quest for Intimate Relatedness," *Contemporary Psychoanalysis* 11, no. 3 (1975).

110   *the best playgrounds have fences*   E. Brown, "Intimacy and Power," *Voices* 15, no. 1 (1979).

    self-disclosure is an important element of an intimate relationship S. Jourard, *The Transparent Self* (New York: Van Nostrand, 1964).

    the capacity to be alone   Donald Winnicott, "The Capacity to Be Alone," *International Journal of Psychoanalysis* 39 (1958).

111   *escalate, stagnate, or deteriorate*   I. Altman, A. Vinsel, and B. B. Brown, "Dialectical Conceptions in Social Psychology," in *Advances in Experimental Social Psychology*, vol. 24, ed. L. Berkowitz (New York: Academic Press, 1981).

    two solitudes protect   R. M. Rilke, *Letters to a Young Poet* (New York: Norton, 1954).

114   *the stresses and frustrations of living together*   Paul C. Rosenblatt and Linda Budd, "Territoriality and Privacy in Married and Unmarried Cohabiting Couples," *Journal of Social Psychology* 97 (1975).

a backstage region for being alone Erving Goffman, *The Presentation of Self in Everyday Life* (New York: Anchor, 1959).

115 *expectations are often not met because* Sandra Petronio, "Communication Boundary Management: Managing Disclosure of Private Information Between Marital Couples," *Communication Theory* 1, no. 4 (1991).

they are frequently not understood Deborah Tannen, *You Just Don't Understand: Women and Men in Conversation* (New York: Ballantine, 1991).

116 *what's inside a relationship* Wendy M. Williams and Michael Barnes, "Love Within Life," in *The Psychology of Love*, eds. Robert J. Sternberg and Michael Barnes (New Haven: Yale University Press, 1988).

117 *the latter that makes the former possible* Joseph Pleck and Jack Sawyer, *Men and Masculinity* (Englewood Cliffs, N.J.: Spectrum, 1974).

118 *greater involvement on the part of women* Robert J. Sternberg and S. Grajek, "The Nature of Love," *Journal of Personality and Social Psychology* 47 (1984).

119 *married people tend to have less permeable boundaries* Hartmann, op. cit.

120 *indexes of boundaries between partners* D. Baucom, N. Epstein, L. Rankin, and C. Burnett, "Assessing Relationship Standards: The Inventory of Specific Relationship Standards," *Journal of Family Psychology* 10, no. 1 (1966).

one of the most significant dimensions in marital satisfaction Pauline Boss, "The Marital Relationship: Boundaries and Ambiguities," in *Stress and the Family, Volume 1: Coping with Normative Family Transitions*, eds. H. I. McCubbin and C. R. Figley (New York: Bruner/Mazel, 1983).

122 *guilty of self betrayal* R. D. Laing, *Self and Others* (Baltimore: Penguin, 1969).

the unconscious trading off of mutual projections Maggie Scarf, *Intimate Partners* (New York: Random House, 1987).

the I within the We M. Karpel, "Individuation: From Fusion to Dialogue," *Family Process* 15 (1976).

Chapter 7. Where You End and He (or She) Begins

128 *power tends to follow the money* Pepper Schwartz, *Love Between Equals: How Peer Marriage Really Works* (New York: Free Press, 1995).

134 *patterns in how couples regulate distance*   Karpel, op. cit.

137 *the validator adaptation*   John Gottman, *Why Marriages Succeed or Fail* (New York: Simon & Schuster, 1996).

141 *boundary ambiguity is one of the biggest fault lines*   Pauline Boss, op. cit.

Chapter 8. Social Bonds and Boundaries

149 *the community of familiar strangers*   Marvin Thomas, *The Personal Village* (Seattle: Hara Publishing, 2003).

   the difference between community and attachment   Robert Weiss, *Loneliness: The Experience of Social Isolation* (Cambridge, Mass.: MIT Press, 1974).

150 *we find them in*   Hartmann, op. cit.

151 *the social exchange theory*   Graham A. Allan, *A Sociology of Friendship and Kinship* (London: Allen & Unwin, 1979).

153 *the interpersonal stage*   Kegan, op. cit.

155 *the end rather than the means*   Kegan, op. cit.

156 *with quantum physics*   Popp, op. cit.

157 *convenience friends*   Viorst, op. cit.

159 *Betrayal is the terrorism of friendship*   Pogrebin, op. cit.

160 *a total loss of self*   Jean Baker Miller, *Toward a New Psychology of Women* (Boston: Beacon Press, 1987).

Chapter 9. Who Can You Call at Three in the Morning?

174 *an exchange of selflessness*   Karin Schultz, "Women's Adult Development: The Importance of Friendship," *Journal of Independent Social Work* 5, no. 2 (1991).

   not only preserve but also strengthen it   Jean Baker Miller, *Women's Growth in Connection: Writings from the Stone Center* (Wellesley, Mass.: Stone Center for Research on Women, 1991).

   in the context of important relationships   Carl Rogers, *On Becoming a Person* (Boston: Houghton Mifflin, 1961).

175 *the realities of the relationship*   Lillian Rubin, *Just Friends* (New York: HarperCollins, 1985).

Chapter 10. In and Out of Bounds at the Office

181 *As Hartmann pointed out*   Hartmann, op. cit.

184 *support, and marital satisfaction*   Michael Leiter and Marie Durup, "Work, Home and in Between: A Longitudinal Study of Spillover," *Journal of Applied Behavioral Science* 32, no. 1 (1996).

the dynamics of work and family boundaries operate similarly   Michael Frone, Marcia Russell, and M. Lynne Cooper, "Prevalence of Work/Family Conflict: Are Work and Family Boundaries Asymmetrically Permeable?" *Journal of Organizational Behavior* 13, no. 7 (1992).

188 *acting like a boss in front of friends*   David Koeppel, "A Tough Transition: Friend to Supervisor," *New York Times*, March 16, 2003.

189 *status in the organization was roughly equal*   Kennan Bridge and Leslie A. Baxter, "Blended Relationships: Friends As Work Associates," *Western Journal of Communication* 56, no. 3 (1992).

work can often lead   Pogrebin, op. cit.

198 *the organization's boundaries*   Tom Tyler and Roderick Kramer, *Trust in Organizations: Frontiers of Theory and Research* (New York: Sage Publications, 1995).

201 *cooperate effectively across organizational boundaries*   Michelle Williams, "Seeing through the Client's Eyes: Building Interpersonal Trust, Cooperation and Performance Across Organizational Boundaries (Ph.D. thesis, Ann Arbor: University of Michigan, 2002).

Index